Collection Development in Theological Libraries

Abiding Principles and Emerging Practices

EDITED BY CARISSE MICKEY BERRYHILL

ATLA OPEN PRESS

Chicago – 2022

atla Open Press

Published by Atla Open Press, an imprint of the American Theological Library Association (Atla), 200 South Wacker Drive, Suite 3100, Chicago, IL 60606-6701 USA

Published in the United States of America in 2022

ISBN-13 978-1-949800-31-9 (PDF)
ISBN-13 978-1-949800-32-6 (EPUB)
ISBN-13 978-1-949800-33-3 (Paperback)

Cover design by Simply Aesthetic

Contents

Emerging Practices

Foreword

T HE THEOLOGICAL LIBRARIAN'S HANDBOOK IS A MULTI-VOLUME INTRODUCTORY and concise guide to theological librarianship intended for library staff who do not possess formal training in the field of library and information science, do not have access to it, or are unable to acquire it in a formal way. Such library staff can often be found in small and emerging theological libraries in the majority world, but also in church and monastery libraries in the West. They are mostly solo librarians with a degree in theology or similar degree in humanities who have been instructed in their job responsibilities by another member of the institution or by an external professional librarian.

This book series is a project of the International Theological Li- brarianship Education initiative (ITLE), an international effort by members of four theological library associations (Atla, ANZTLA, BETH, and ForAtl) created in 2018. The mission of ITLE is to strengthen and connect theological and religious studies librarians worldwide by identifying resources, creating educational opportunities, and developing skill enhancement materials through collaborative efforts. The idea to produce a book series on the practice of theological librarianship came because of discussions within the task force about the state of theological librarianship world-wide and the understanding that many theological librarians are working in isolation, without access to any form of professional training or support from colleagues.

There are many reasons these librarians do not have professional training today:

- **no access**—the absence of library science programs or library professionals in their working area, or, if a program is available, it is delivered in such a manner that a working librarian is unable to attend classes;

- **too expensive**—in many countries, a professional or master's degree in library science can be very expensive, and the theological librarians or their libraries cannot afford to pay for training;

- **no legal status**—in some countries, religious libraries do not have a clear and recognized status. They are not mentioned in any of the country's laws and standards for libraries, nor do they have a section in their national library associations. Therefore, there is no overarching national institution or law that would require library staff in these libraries to have a professional degree. This is mostly the case with theological libraries belonging to religious communities;

- **no organizations**—the absence of professional theological library associations in a country or region that would organize theological library education workshops and seminars;

- **no motivation**—some institutions to which these libraries belong believe that professional training for work in a theological library is not necessary.

Because of all these reasons, members of ITLE decided to develop various freely accessible synchronous and asynchronous means of library education which will be offered to the international theological library community. This handbook series is one of those means and is primarily addressed to librarians in smaller, more independent libraries, which are not part of university libraries or systems. These would include libraries of seminaries, churches, institutes, etc. Librarians working in such libraries usually have more freedom to implement their own policies and practices but may not be well equipped to formulate them. The handbook seeks to address the most important topics and challenges for their work and give advice on these matters.

This third volume in the handbook series explores why and how theological librarians build collections of resources. The first five chapters examine **abiding principles** that can guide the decisions librarians make about the materials they select, with special emphasis on diversity, equity, inclusion, and antiracism. Often the guidelines for decision-making are expressed in a policy document, a basic tool mentioned often throughout the book. Authors in this first group of essays pay particular attention to how collection policy is decided, what the key components of that policy should be, and how the policy functions.

The next six chapters focus on **emerging practices** applied to developing particular types of collections in local settings, often using a case description to illustrate. Beginning with an overview of building a collection from the ground up, this section then explores collection assessment, reference collections, special collections, the impact of the pandemic on libraries' uptake of electronic collections, and collaborative resource development. Each author strives to offer methods that are financially feasible for the intended readers of the handbook.

The international authors of these chapters are quite focused on the purpose of the theological library to serve its constituents with usable and accessible resources, as Jeremy Wallace phrases it in Chapter 1. Their common ethos of hospitable stewardship and service abides even when libraries grapple with seismic shifts in their educational, financial, technological, religious, cultural, and political contexts. The good news is that they understand the enduring wisdom of cooperation locally, regionally, and worldwide to meet those challenges.

We hope that this open access volume will provide guidance and a sense of community to its readers, whatever their library setting. We are each and all engaged in the noble work of understanding our communities in order to serve their information needs. We invite our readers to think along with us about how to fulfill our calling.

Matina Ćurić (series editor)
Carisse Mickey Berryhill (volume editor)

Abiding Principles

CHAPTER 1

Creating a Useful, Accessible, & Connected Theological Library

JEREMY WALLACE

T HIS ESSAY SEEKS TO PROVIDE SOME GUIDANCE FOR DEVELOPING A THEOLOGICAL library when resources are few. The hope is that the principles outlined here will also be of benefit to those libraries where resources may be more plentiful. Earlier measures of the health of a library's collection centered on its size, but a more helpful criterion today is the collection's use. How is the collection supporting the research and curricular needs of its institution? Are researchers able to find what they need, regardless of the size of the library? A useful library does not need to be a large library, but it does need to be developed with its users, or researchers, in mind. The good news here is that endless resources are not necessary to create a functional and excellent theological library. The challenge is that a well-used theological library must be developed in such a way that it is indeed useful to its researchers. This involves providing access to foundational and authoritative resources and being aware of the particular research and curricular needs of the institution's faculty and students. Beyond use, two other criteria should be considered when developing a theological collection: access and partnerships. Access is important in many contexts but became especially pronounced during the pandemic when researchers were sometimes cut off even from their own institution's physical library. Partnerships are helpful in providing additional avenues for access and for deferring the acquisition of materials that might not be needed in perpetuity by the home institution. By focusing on use, access, and partnerships, it should be possible to create a strong theological library, even when resources are limited.

A Useful Library

The ongoing development of a theological collection can take many different forms. Some libraries have seemingly limitless resources and are able to follow a just-in-case model of acquisition where books and other media are acquired before any request is made from the researcher. There, acquisitions anticipate future use. Popular methods for developing a just-in-case library collection are approval plans and standing orders. Few libraries can follow this model anymore. Other libraries need to be more careful with their limited resources and must follow a just-in-time model of acquisition where books or other media are acquired on the basis of requests from the researcher. There, acquisitions are generated by actual use. Such libraries are often reliant on borrowing material from other libraries or purchasing it promptly if possible. The just-in-case library is likely to be quite large and the just-in-time library small, but the size of the collection does not determine how good a collection is. For that, it is necessary to understand how any collection is used.

It is unlikely that readers are coming to this article looking for specific titles of books or other resources to add to their theological collections. Many theological collections have the same building blocks: scriptural commentaries; dictionaries, handbooks, and encyclopedias; lexical and grammatical aids for the study of ancient languages; primary sources in the original languages and/or translation; and authoritative monographs. What exactly to purchase necessarily involves the very important question of use. Who will be using these resources, and how? This will affect both resource selection and format preference.

Perhaps the sharpest distinction is between research use and curricular use. The former involves supporting the pursuit of a highly specialized topic with the end goal of adding something new to the scholarly record. The latter is closely tied to the instructional function of the institution. There, it is important to build a theological collection that can support the pedagogical vision of the institution. Research needs are often individual, meaning the resources will only need to be consulted once or by only one person. Curricular needs are often communal, meaning that many students will often be consulting the same resources.

Research and curricular needs can be mapped often, but not always, to faculty and students respectively, because the information needs of theological faculty and students are generally defined by the expected output of their research. Faculty research tends to be done to prepare for courses or to produce scholarship for tenure or career progression (Wenderoth 2007; Cooper and Schonfeld 2017). Very little research is done by faculty for the sole purpose of curiosity; promotions, honors, and reputation are often dependent upon publishing in the right journals and with the most prestigious publishers. For students, course syllabi and assignments usually define the scope of that research (Lincoln and Lincoln 2011). Students attempt to research whatever is necessary to complete the assignment, and often only that.

Between the two, research needs are those that likely cannot be substituted. If a resource is needed for research, either that particular item will need to be found or its absence will be a gap in the research. For curricular needs, there may be a preference for a particular resource, but this, even with difficulty (and possibly great grumbling from the faculty member), can likely be replaced with a different reading.

The greatest challenge for developing a theological library is to support the research activity of its most demanding researchers. Faculty have been trained (rightly) that it is important to consult the relevant literature before making new authoritative claims in their fields. The good news, if it can be called that, is that faculty have avenues other than the library to support their research. Many faculty do their research from home, not at the library, as Wenderoth (2007, 180) confirms: "No one, no one, no one goes to the seminary library to begin their research." There appear to be three primary reasons why this is the case: a desire to avoid distractions, preferred discovery behaviors, and personal collections and libraries. First, faculty avoid going to the library in order to avoid running into students or other distractions. As Wenderoth observes, "The seminary library is a landmine strewn with pesky students" (179). Second, as already noted, the preferred entry into a research topic initially for faculty is not found at the library. Instead, they rely on their informal network of colleagues and other information sources (Gorman 1990; Michels 2005; Wenderoth 2007; Penner 2009), or they search on the web, using some combination of sites like Google and Amazon (Wenderoth 2007; Cooper and Schonfeld 2017). Finally, many faculty simply rely on their own personal collections and libraries, instead of the institutional library (Gorman 1990; Penner 2009; Cooper and Schonfeld 2017). Personal collections are just as, if not more, important than institutional collections (Gorman 1990). Since research can be so specialized, some scholars may have better personal collections and libraries with respect to their topic than the library's collections at their academic institutions. "Religious studies scholars develop significant information collections over the course of their careers and these activities are generally unmediated by their institutions or informational professionals" (Cooper and Schonfeld 2017, 37). Still, the library has an important role to play in helping faculty to locate and access materials that might otherwise be unavailable to them.

Contrary to the exacting research demands of faculty, most theological libraries can naturally support the curricular needs of the institution, or those resources can often be located without too much difficulty. The world tends to be awash in older commentaries, bibles, and authoritative monographs that can be used to support curriculum. The challenges here are related to acquiring materials for interdisciplinary topics or new courses, where acquisitions beyond the typical collecting scope are required.

Library access to resources should not dictate research or curriculum, but at times this is unavoidable, especially when hard-to-locate resources cannot be sourced in a fiscally responsible way. At other times, lack of access is also unforeseeable, as happened to many libraries starting in early 2020.

An Accessible Library

The pandemic disruptions and shutdowns made one thing very clear: collection development is also about access, or, at the very least, the two are inextricably linked. What this looked like for many was that the library's local print collection was inaccessible or, at least, access was limited for a time; ILL was suspended; partners who formerly provided reciprocal borrowing needed to focus on the safety of their own communities first; books were being published, but not shipped or cataloged; or, conversely, books were not being published. The somewhat free flow of information was suddenly interrupted. It is hard to imagine that many could have foreseen this disruption.

Much of this disruption was due to this fact: print still dominates the theological world, at least insofar as researcher preference and publication models are concerned. In general, theological faculty and students consistently show a preference for books over other information sources (Gorman 1990; Penned 2009; Lincoln and Lincoln 2011; Gaba and Ganski 2011). "Theologians want books on shelves, and this has implications not only for how theological librarians function but also how strongly they lobby for improved acquisitions budgets for both current and retrospective collection development" (Gorman 1990, 155). Theological students are "quite book and print bound" (Penner 2009, 66). What the pandemic made evident is that even the local holdings of a library may not be fully utilized when access is restricted.

When it became more difficult to handle physical items during the pandemic, access to theological collections suffered, and so too did research possibilities and use. One thing that kept me up at night was thinking about all of the books, articles, dissertations, and other scholarly outputs that simply were not being advanced due to a lack of access to the necessary resources.

One of the easiest ways to pandemic-proof a collection is through the acquisition of digital resources. There are tremendous digital resources available now to aid in the study of theology and its related disciplines. The most-used database at my institution is Atla Religion Database with Atla Serials Plus. This database provides easy search across a number of full text journals. Its distinguishing feature from other EBSCO databases is the ability to search using the Scriptures Index. It is hard to imagine a theological library that would not find this product to be useful. These Atla databases can also be made accessible to libraries in developing countries through subsidies or through the sponsorship of other institutions.

There are also growing digital initiatives that can provide access to theological content. Atla Digital Library, Theological Commons (Princeton Theological Seminary's digital library), and the

Digital Theological Library are some examples among a crowded field. Other good news is that mass digitization is increasingly making both out-of-copyright and even copyrighted material available for researchers. When print collections became inaccessible due to the pandemic, many libraries turned to HathiTrust to gain digital access to books they held in print. Internet Archive has also been a strong leader in making resources more widely available to anyone with an internet connection. If a resource is not available locally, it is important (and often rewarding) to check whether the resource has already been digitized and is available somewhere online. Beyond those mentioned above, Google Books and Amazon's Look Inside feature can sometimes provide the needed window of information. There are countless other freely available resources online for finding material that might be useful to theological faculty and students.

A newer model used by libraries to leverage their legacy print collections is controlled digital lending, the process of making a digital copy of a print book available on an owned-to-loaned ratio. This is especially useful for those books that have not been digitized and made accessible digitally to institutions by publishers or aggregate vendors. Further good news is that CDL does not only benefit the library digitizing the copy. It is possible for libraries with fewer resources to take advantage of the digitalization done by other libraries to gain access to the needed information.

Another way of providing database access to certain individuals is through negotiating for alumni access. This often comes at an additional cost, but not always. It may be that faculty of an institution are able to gain access to additional electronic databases through their alma mater. This may be one more way that the research needs of theological faculty can be satisfied.

Finally, evidence-based acquisition models are especially useful because they provide access, generally, to a publisher's full catalog of e-books for an up-front deposit amount that will then be applied to the perpetual purchase of resources at the end of the EBA period. This is a good way to use limited resources to acquire materials that have been used, based on analytics. What makes this model preferable over the earlier patron-driven acquisition or demand-driven acquisition models is that the actual purchase decision is still made by the librarian who can think about how such a perpetual purchase would help to shape the collection for the future.

While this wealth of digital options is promising, and some will argue that it is possible to create a fully digital theological library now, the publisher market just is not there yet. That the Anchor Bible Dictionary and Commentaries were only very recently made available digitally to institutions is a sign of how much backlist material still remains to be offered in that format. There are many other titles that I as a collection development librarian would love to purchase for my library in digital format but cannot, because print is still the only format option for so many publications in theology and related disciplines. The other challenge from a publishing point of view is that the more popular a title is, the less likely it is to be made available digitally on an unlimited-user access model. The publisher will want the institution to buy multiple single-user access copies. Perhaps some day the publishing models will change, and theological literature will be more widely available digitally. Then, it will be necessary to convince researchers that the digital format gives them benefits over the print and that they should shift their reading preferences there. For now, "digital research is both ubiquitous and marginal," or, in other words, "everyone" is doing it, but not everyone is doing it well (Cooper and Schonfeld 2017, 35).

It is hard to imagine a better collection than one where all research was accessible and could be retrieved simply at the request of a researcher. Increased digitization is making some of this a reality, but the goal is still well in the future. Having discussed both use and access, the final proposal for those seeking to build theological collections is to think about building better connections.

A Connected Library

The future of library collections has been trending toward cooperative collection development—the belief that no library collection can be comprehensive enough to be fully independent and that partnerships are necessary. This is true even of very large libraries, as evidenced by the collections at ReCAP (provided by Princeton University, Columbia University, New York Public Library, and Harvard University) and Ivy Plus that can ferry resources quickly between some of the best libraries in the world. Libraries, recognizing the deficiencies inherent in any attempt at self-sufficiency, have sought partnerships through consortia, regional partners, collectives, and other models for resource sharing. The resource sharing model used by almost all libraries is interlibrary loan, but local and regional partnerships have also been important.

Use and access can help you to determine what to buy for your library; partnerships can help you decide what you do not need to buy. It is time for libraries to begin considering a connection development policy if there is not one already in place. What strategic partners can help to advance access to useful resources? Where might there be a mutually beneficial relationship where both partners are able to extend their collections by having access to one another's? This is both a judicious use of resources and a way to access more with less.

Since the primary purpose of this article is to give some basic guidelines for building a theological collection with limited resources, I reached out to Wayne Bornholdt, director of acquisitions at the Theological Book Network (TBN) to discuss resource acquisition for such libraries. TBN has been a partner to many of them. As stated on their website, "[TBN] ship[s] high-quality theological resources to under-resourced theological schools in Africa, Asia, Latin America, Eastern Europe, and the Middle East." TBN is often contracted by foundations or churches who have schools that they want to support by building theological collections there. TBN receives donations of in-scope theological books (these include books on certain subjects published in the last 30 years) and matches their inventory to the requests of the destination institution. Even when TBN might not be able to provide specific books, they can often provide alternatives and support subject collections broadly. This is likely the easiest way for an institution with limited resources to create a theological collection: by partnering with a donor and using TBN's services. Well-resourced theological libraries have a role to play in this cycle by donating unneeded books that fit TBN's scope. This partnership among TBN, well-resourced libraries, and under-resourced libraries can help to redistribute theological resources where they are needed most.

The pandemic and the uncertainty caused by it frustrated many partnerships. Some researchers had trouble accessing their own library's collections, let alone the collections of other libraries. This predicament suggests that cooperative collection development alone will not be enough to ensure continued access to important resources. Even now, well into the third year of the pandemic, some libraries are closed to those outside their immediate community, making partnerships and resource sharing even more difficult.

Difficulties do not mean, however, that these efforts should cease, but that partnerships should be strengthened and that continued access should be a priority. Many libraries have already become adept at giving limited access to their print collections through curbside delivery and scanning services. Such practices will make it easier to provide access should lockdowns be needed again in the future.

Conclusion

Use, access, and connections inform and support the development of theological libraries. It is in the best interest of all theological libraries (those more and less resourced) to focus on those three issues when developing such a collection. Does your library meet the needs of its users? Are the collections accessible? Have you established partnerships to provide further access to resources to meet your users' needs? Exploring these three questions can help those libraries then prioritize which resources need to be bought and which can be borrowed from other partners. The best theological collection is one that will be useful and accessible to its patrons. Partnerships provide other access points for resources outside of the collecting scope or budgetary constraints of the library. The truth is that all libraries have limited resources, even if these limits are large. The theological record is simply too great for any one library to collect on its own.

Works Cited

Cooper, D., & Schonfeld, R. 2017. "Supporting the Changing Research Practices of Religious Studies Scholars." *Ithaka S+R*, February 8. *https://doi.org/10.18665/sr.294119*.

Gaba, R., & Ganski, K. 2011. "The CATLA Study: Reading, Researching, and Writing Habits of Master of Divinity Students and the Role the Library Plays in These Processes, a Study of Methods and Environments." In *American Theological Library Association Summary Of Proceedings* 65: 122–52.

Gorman, G. E. 1990. "Patterns of Information Seeking and Library Use by Theologians in Seven Adelaide Theological Colleges." *Australian Academic & Research Libraries* 21: 137–56.

Lincoln, T. D., & Lincoln, L. M. 2011. "From Intention to Composition: How Seminarians Conceptualize Research." *Theological Librarianship* 4, no. 1: 41–67.

Michels, D. H. 2005. "The Use of People as Information Sources in Biblical Studies Research." *Canadian Journal of Information & Library Sciences* 29, no. 1: 91–109.

Penner, K. 2009. "Information Needs and Behaviours of Theology Students at the International Baptist Theological Seminary." *Theological Librarianship* 2, no. 2: 51–80.

Wenderoth, C. 2007. "Research Behaviors of Theological Educators and Students: The Known and the Unknown." In *American Theological Library Association Summary Of Proceedings* 61: 178–83.

CHAPTER 2

Care and Tending of the Garden

The Collection Management Policy as Gardening Manual

LESLIE A. ENGELSON

I N 1931, S. R. Ranganathan developed five laws that define a library's functions and responsibilities. The fifth law, "the library is a growing organism" (Ranganathan 1931, 382) encourages the use of a garden as a metaphor for library collections. Gardens, like library collections, are in a perpetual state of change and adjustment. They are never finished and need constant and consistent tending in order to thrive and benefit their users. This chapter envisions the collection management policy as a gardening manual that guides the library director as they tend the library's collections.

Whether a garden or a library collection, the health of either is determined by its ability for growth and flexibility. As with gardens, if a collection is not well tended, it will die or become of limited use to the community it serves. Gardening manuals provide information for the gardener to help them make decisions that will ensure positive growth and development of the garden for its users. Likewise, in order to have a library collection that is useful for the community that it serves, management of the library's collection should be guided by a well developed collection management policy.

To clarify, throughout this chapter, when the term *collection* is used in the singular form, it is referring to all the collections available in and through the library.

Purpose

The collection management policy (CMP) is a document that guides the collection management decisions of the library staff to serve both the present and future needs of the library user. CMPs help the library director know where to focus attention and funds in order to steward the library's collection in a thoughtful and balanced way. It provides library staff the opportunity to codify collection development decisions in a systematic and thoughtful way. It states the mission of the library, the purpose the library serves, and provides continuity across time and personnel changes.

Because the CMP allows for transparency and communicates what the library is about, it should be published on the library's website. In essence, a CMP contains guidelines for making decisions that address the who, what, when, where, why, and how of the library's collection.

- Who?

    ° Whom do the collections serve?

    ° Who makes the final decisions for selection and deselection?

- What?

    ° What types of resources are collected?

    ° What is the goal for the level of coverage?

    ° What criteria are used for selection and deselection?

- Where?
  - Where are resources that are sensitive or costly located?
  - Where is equipment stored?
  - Where are formats other than print materials located?
- When?
  - When is the CMP reviewed and revised?
  - When are collections inventoried and assessed?
- Why?
  - Why are resources selected?
  - Why are resources deselected?
- How?
  - How are the collections organized?
  - How are resources purchased?
  - How is access provided?
  - How are challenges handled?
  - How are the collections assessed?

The CMP is usually created by the library director collaboratively with staff, informed by the community they serve, and is approved and endorsed by either a person or committee that oversees the work of the library and library director. This endorsement is important as it conveys support by the larger governing body for the library director and serves as a means of protection should questions arise about decisions and actions they make.

Context

Most gardens are not designed or built in a haphazard way with little consideration of the context in which they exist. Rather, the context determines the type of plants that are grown in the garden, whether the garden is ornamental or used for growing food, is in pots or raised beds, and so forth. In the same way, the context in which a library exists determines the types of resources to which that library provides access and how the resources are organized and accessed. The context in which library collections function consists of three elements:

1. The community served

2. The curriculum supported

3. The collections developed

Community

The degree to which the library's collection is responsive to the community it serves is correlative to how well the community's information needs are served by that library. As noted in Berryhill's (2020, 8) explanation of what theological libraries are, "theological libraries vary in their constituencies." Yet all academic libraries serve two distinct communities to one degree or another: internal communities and external communities.

Internal community members are the people served directly by the institution: congregants, clergy, students, faculty, staff, and administration. Members of the internal community are the primary users of the library collection. Therefore, it should reflect the diversity of those members.

Some elements that provide a cursory understanding of the complexity of the internal community include demographics such as age, ethnic background, socioeconomic level, education level, religious affiliation, and grade point average. Furthermore, knowing whether students reside on campus or commute, the length of commute, and the prevalence and reliability of internet access for internal community members, particularly those who commute, is helpful. Another element to consider is the percentage of the internal community members who are international and what their primary language may be.

An often-overlooked element of understanding the internal community is knowing who is not coming to the library or using the library's resources and why, so that collections can be built or resources added that target these community members to draw them in.

The makeup of the external community is informed by the mission of the institution. Some theological libraries are quite restrictive in the types of users they allow to access their resources beyond the internal community, and their external community may consist only of those users served through interlibrary loan and consortial agreements. Other theological libraries make their collections available to anyone who walks through the doors. These external community members may include physical neighbors to the institution, local clergy and theological scholars, volunteers, members of friends-of-the-library groups, alumni, and institutional governance members.

Interests, strengths, and challenges in each community also should be noted as well as annual, seasonal, and other special community events.

Community members can also serve as resources for support and assistance. Collaborative partnerships developed with constituents within both the internal and external communities can serve to advise, inform, mentor, and support the work of the library and its director. Volunteers are a well-known asset but are not the only community members who can partner with the library. Knowing the extent of resources available in both internal and external communities and building relationships with decision-makers and those who hold the purse strings can greatly benefit the library.

Finally, communities are in a constant state of change. They shrink and grow. People come and go. Local, regional, national, and even global events can impact a community. There is no community that stays constant forever. Even if the library director has a sense of what the communities the library serves are like today, they will likely be different in three, four, or five years. Regular assessment of both communities informs the mission, goals, and strategic plan.

A summary of the characteristics of both the internal and external communities will be included in the CMP. This summary should be updated when assessments are completed.

Curriculum

Theological libraries exist to support and supplement the curriculum of the institutions with which they are associated. Therefore, it is incumbent upon the library director and other library personnel who make collection decisions to be aware of the curriculum provided by the institution by serving on curriculum committees. Attending department meetings also informs selectors of changes to curriculum and programs that are added or cut so decisions can be made that are responsive to these changes.

It is helpful to work in partnership with faculty on major research projects they assign their students to ensure sufficient resources are available to meet the demand. Likewise, meeting with the clergy on a regular basis to learn about upcoming sermon series or topics enables library directors of congregational libraries to proactively provide resources that supplement sermon themes.

Theological libraries situated within institutions that offer a curriculum that is broader than theology, religion, and ministry provide access to resources that support the entire curriculum. Libraries situated within institutions with curriculum limited to theology, religion, and ministry still need to provide access to resources that cover more generalized subject areas—just to a lesser degree—or ensure that their internal community has access to these resources through a local library.

Libraries should also consider providing resources that support extra-curricular activities available on campus such as film screenings, conferences, and locally produced podcasts. It is helpful to connect with the appropriate offices to find out about both institution- and student-initiated extra-curricular activities.

A library director should also be aware of the curriculum initiatives and trends impacting higher education, such as distance learning and pedagogical trends, in order to provide proactive acquisition of resources.

A brief summary of the topical foci of the curriculum, whether formal or informal, will be included in the CMP.

Collection

In order to develop a collection that meets the information and interest needs of the community and curriculum, the library director needs to assess the current collection, determining what resources are available, where the gaps are, and how effective it is. Collection analysis looks at the strengths and weaknesses of the collection as it relates to the community and the curriculum and considers the criteria included in the CMP for selection and deselection.

The library director should also be aware of resources available through other libraries. For instance, consortial agreements often include the use of physical items from other libraries through interlibrary loan. Consortial agreements can also include shared purchasing of both physical and electronic resources. The director should also consider whether internal community members have access to other library's collections that are in close proximity to them.

Assessing the organization of the library is a crucial element to understanding the collection. Commonly, a theological library's resources are loosely sorted by format into collections such as reference, circulating, periodicals, audio-visual, electronic resources, and sometimes equipment. Some libraries also include separate collections for archives, maps, and rare materials.

Physical collections are organized by a system that is often determined based on the format of the resource. For instance, periodical collections are often organized by title, fiction collections are organized by either author last name or genre, and reference and circulating collections are usually organized by a classification system such as the Library of Congress Classification System or the Dewey Decimal Classification System. Electronic databases are usually organized on the library's web pages by topic or subject.

A brief description of each collection of the library, formats collected, and how the collections are organized should be included in the CMP.

Elements of a Collection Management Policy

To grow a garden, some foundational elements are soil, sun, and water. Additional elements—such as seeds and compost—and actions—such as staking, pruning, and weeding—all contribute to a thriving garden that serves the gardener well. Similarly, the CMP contains elements that are fundamental to ensuring a library collection not only grows but thrives and serves the community and curriculum well.

Mission Statement

Like soil, sun, and water to the garden, the library's mission statement is an essential element of the CMP. It should align with the mission of the institution and should reflect the purpose for the library collection's existence. A theological library collection is a means to an end, not an end in itself, and the mission statement helps keep that end in mind. Goals and values are also included to clarify the library's purpose.

Community Profile

The community profile is a brief summary of both the internal and external communities served by the library as well as a statement indicating that the community will be reassessed every three to five years.

Diversity, Equity, and Inclusion

The library's commitment to diversity, equity, and inclusion in the description of, access to, and content of the collection should be clearly stated, as this impacts all facets of collection management. This section should also address support for users regardless of their location and ability.

Collection Management Decisions

While purchase recommendations from faculty, students, and other community members are welcome and encouraged, ideally the library director and subject-specific librarians in larger libraries should have the final determination related to collection management decisions. They know and understand the community, curriculum, and collection, the principles and values of the profession of librarianship, and the criteria used for evaluating resources. The CMP clarifies the advisory role of a governmental body, such as a library committee, and indicates its makeup.

Additionally, information about how the communities served by the library can communicate with the library director, whether that be through suggestion boxes, links on websites, or email addresses or phone numbers, is helpful to include.

Collection Scope

The collection scope is a brief description of the formal and informal curriculum supported by the library followed by a statement about the desired collection goals. This includes what collections the library will have and the types of materials and resources to which the library can provide access. Additionally, state the desired depth of collection in each topical area of the library.

A helpful scale of collection depth developed by the Research Libraries Group and available from the Library of Congress (*loc.gov/acq/devpol/cpc.html*) can be adapted by libraries of any size (Mayer 2018, 9).

Additionally, this section should specify information about the following criteria:

- Curriculum support

- Cost

- Authority

- Accuracy

- Bias/Perspective

- Format

- Age

- Number of copies

- Currency

- Language

- Reading level

- Condition (for physical resources)

Additional criteria related specifically to electronic resources should detail:

- Accessibility

- Usability

- Licensing

- Pricing model (Mangrum 2012, 110)

Finally, the role of open access resources, digitization, and shared repositories in collection development goals should be elucidated.

This information guides and supports both selection and deselection decisions, so it is crucial that it be as specific and thorough as possible. It is also helpful to include statements about collection balance and limiting factors. In the event of a challenge to a resource added to the collection or a concern about resources withdrawn from the collection, a clear statement about the criteria used for selection and deselection decisions can address those challenges and concerns.

Finally, the CMP indicates the scope, frequency, and responsibility of inventories as well as assessments of both physical and electronic resources.

Organization

A brief description of the various collections as well as how they are organized should be included. This will indicate the classification system(s) used along with locally developed organization schemes and the rationale behind their use. The organization and access of electronic resources should also be addressed.

Preservation

A discussion of how physical materials are processed, if they are mended, as well as the process and criteria for deselection should be covered.

Acquisition Responsibilities and Methods

How the purchase of resources is funded, who is responsible for the acquisitions process, how gifts are handled, how recommendations and requests can be made, and how to deal with challenges should be explained in this section.

The library's consideration of acquisition models such as patron-driven acquisitions / demand-driven acquisitions (PDA/DDA), approval plans, standing orders, and subscriptions should also be stated along with summaries of formal consortial agreements.

Intellectual Freedom Statement

Another fundamental element of the CMP is a statement about the responsibility of theological libraries to support intellectual freedom through access to information. This is a professional ethic to which all library directors and librarians subscribe and uphold. It can be challenging within the context of a theological library to reflect the values of the institution and community as well as support access to a variety of viewpoints and perspectives, but it is essential to allow the library user to make their choice about what information they access. Furthermore, it is important to remember that the institution does not need to endorse, agree with, or approve every idea or presentation that the library makes available.

The American Library Association (ALA) has developed a number of statements and policies on access (ALA 2021) which can be referenced in this part of the CMP. If it is too controversial to include the ALA's Library Bill of Rights (*ala.org/advocacy/intfreedom/librarybill*), provide a statement such as: "The Library will uphold its users' right to access and use a variety of information and materials, including controversial information and materials." This should suffice to both clarify the role of the library within the institution as well as support the decisions of the library director and their staff.

Lastly, there should be statements about the role the library director serves as protector of an individual's right to privacy and confidentiality in the use of library resources and services, as well as the user's right to freely express their opinions about library resources and services.

Policy Revision Cycle

While the CMP should be a fairly stable document, regular updates will be informed by changes in the community, curriculum, and collection. Major changes within the institution may also indicate a need to revise the CMP. The CMP should include a timeline for reviewing the CMP on a regular basis as well as indicate who will be involved in the revision process. It is also helpful to indicate the methods used for analyzing the community, curriculum, and collections to facilitate continuity and identify gaps in the analysis.

Conclusion

If written thoughtfully, deliberately, and comprehensively, the CMP will serve the library and its staff as they seek to tend this growing organism for the benefit and use of its community.

Works Cited

American Library Association. 2019. "Library Bill of Rights." *https://ala.org/advocacy/intfreedom/librarybill.*

———. 2021. "Access to Library Resources and Services." *https://ala.org/advocacy/intfreedom/access.*

Berryhill, Carisse Mickey. 2020. "What are Theological Libraries?" In *Introduction to Theological Libraries,* edited by Marie Ćurić, 7–15. Chicago: Atla Open Press. *https://books.atla.com/atlapress/catalog/view/34/41/208.*

Library of Congress. 1997. "Collecting Levels." *https://loc.gov/acq/devpol/cpc.html.*

Mangrum, Suzanne, and Mary Ellen Pozzebon. 2012. "Use of Collection Development Policies in Electronic Resource Management. *Collection Building* 31, no. 3: 108–14.

Mayer, Robert J. 2018. "Theological Librarians and Collection Management: Collaborative Policy Development." *Theological Librarianship* 11, no. 2 :8–11.

Ranganathan, S. R. 1931. *The Five Laws of Library Science.* London: Edward Goldston, Ltd. *https://babel.hathitrust.org/cgi/pt?id=uc1.$b99721&view=1up&seq=13.*

CHAPTER 3

Collection Development Policies for Theological Libraries in the Digital Era

WARD DE PRIL

I N 2011, RICK ANDERSEN PREDICTED THAT "IT SEEMS HIGHLY LIKELY THAT THE very idea of the 'collection' will be overhauled if not obviated over the next ten years, in favor of more dynamic access to a virtually unlimited flow of information products" (215). In Andersen's view, there would still be collections in 2021, but the day-to-day significance of those collections would generally be seen as minimal. Few theological librarians today would confirm the validity of this prediction: creating organized, accessible, and durable collections for researchers and students remains central to the work of the theological library. In the network context, our collections are not disappearing, but they can be made more visible, retrievable and immediately accessible, and thus more valuable and useful than ever before. But the notion of what these collections are is changing, and with it the notion of collection development.

In the last decade, theological libraries have felt the impact of the transition towards a digital network environment. The notion of collection first extended in the 1990s from 'owned' print collections to 'licensed' electronic collections. Undoubtedly this entailed significant adjustments in the areas of acquisition modes, accessibility and preservation, but at the same time both collection types—owned versus licensed—were 'traditional' outcomes of research in the sense that libraries acquire this content from publishers and make it available for their registered users only (outside-in movement). A more profound shift is the increased importance of materials that present an inside-out challenge for the library, such as special collections and institutional output, and materials that are freely accessible on the Web (Dempsey 2014, 402). Especially the latter type of materials mean that the scope of the collection is no longer defined by any single location or site but is extended to "a cloud of distributed resources in a variety of places around the globe that are made centrally available via the library" (Horava 2010, 151). The new collection directions challenge the traditional collection-building assumptions of permanence, control, and relative comprehensiveness, and urge us to reformulate our practices of selecting, acquiring, and/or giving access to collections (143).

Before the breakthrough of the digital network environment, collection development was the core task of academic libraries: they aspired to acquire all literature on all aspects of their discipline and did not fundamentally cooperate with other libraries in terms of collection development. Collection development policies have their origins in this print era. Libraries started to develop formal collection development policies in the 1960s, when budget fluctuations and management pressures made them look more closely at their priorities (Vickery 2004, 337). In 1979, the American Library Association Collection Development Committee issued "Guidelines for Collection Development" to support libraries in creating useful and effective collection development policies. In 1989 and 1996, these guidelines were updated and published as the "Guide for Written Collection Development Policy Statements." Its conspectus model was the standard of proactive and well-planned collection building, providing a framework for describing the collection in terms of current and intended levels of collection in specific subject classes. Five collecting levels are identified in the conspectus—minimal, basic, study, research, and comprehensive (Van Zijl 1998, 104). The main issue was to guarantee a balanced collection with regard to subjects in accordance with the library's mission and the expectations of its user body. The conspectus model is still relevant today to guide the selection of content—provided the library continues to uphold a just-in-case purchasing policy—but has to be complemented with policies addressing the shifts in collection development today.

In the late 1990s, the importance of updating written collection development policies was emphasized in view of the integration of electronic resources, which were growing very rapidly. In 2001, the International Federation of Library Associations and Institutions (IFLA) issued its "Guidelines for a Collection Development Policy Using the Conspectus Model," taking into account the need to deal more adequately with non-print and electronic forms of information and access/ownership issues in collection development. But, since 1996 (ALA guide) and 2001 (IFLA guidelines), no such guides have been published that take into account the development and changes in the landscape of scholarly communication and publishing over the last two decades. Nonetheless, given the complexity and variety of collections today, the need for a collection development policy as a decision-making tool seems as evident as a business plan for a business (cf. Johnson 2009, 72). The reasons listed by IFLA in 2001 for investing in a written policy on collection development are still valid in the era of a digital network environment: (1) providing guidance in selecting and deselecting resources, (2) underpinning of future planning, thereby assisting in determining priorities for allocation of budgets, (3) supporting public relations towards stakeholders, and (4) serving as a basis for wider cooperation, even internationally (IFLA 2001, 1–2).

It is not our intention to give a detailed overview of what a collection development policy should look like today. This will vary greatly depending on the mission and goals of the library and the needs of its users. But there are some things that are best included. First of all, an introductory section explains the mission and goals of the library. It remains interesting to add here a history of the collection, its strengths and gaps, and the desired levels of collection depth and breadth. Here it is important to clarify the concept of 'collection' and to indicate which materials can be considered as potential components of the collection, e.g., specific types of open access materials or research data. The main part of the collection development policy should not consist in detailed guidelines for selection, acquisition, weeding etc., but should define fundamental options of the library with regard to such things as format (electronic or print), acquisition models, allocation of budget, digitization priorities, and accessibility for each of the defined collection components.

For an academic library in theology, a subdivision in collection types could be useful to structure a collection development policy: published, purchased, and licensed materials; open access collections (including institutional output); and heritage/legacy collections.

Published, Purchased, and Licensed Materials

This collection type concerns the traditional outcome of research, published in books or journals and acquired by libraries according to the outside-in model. Some crucial and highly interrelated issues that should be discussed in the collection development policy are the print-to-electronic shift, the preferred acquisition models, and preservation implications.

The print-to-electronic shift in libraries clearly needs to be strategized and managed explicitly (cf. Pinfield 2017, 24). Theological libraries do not necessarily want to move to an entirely electronic research collection. Print can be considered important to allow serendipitous discovery through browsing or can have other attributes that make print superior to electronic versions (Douglas 2011, 19). For instance, print is cheaper to purchase, provides better guarantees of long-term preservation, and is better suited for reflective or intense reading. Still, it is important that the policy of the library provides a clear direction and a basis for action. A policy could be to acquire reference works, handbooks, e-textbooks, collected essays, conference proceedings, and festschrifts in an electronic version if available, while scholarly monographs are purchased in print (paperback for economic reasons), just as religious art books, which are not well suited for an electronic format. Major text editions can be purchased in both print and electronic format, as to allow for both text mining and intense reading.

There are a variety of acquisition models and each library should consider which model best suits its mission: does the library fulfill the function of a general acquirer in the field of theology (just-in-case collection building) or is it mainly a user library (just-in-time collection building)? Does the library have a preservation function or not? Depending on the answers to these questions, the library will choose whether to subscribe to journals in print or to license them singly or collaboratively ('big deals'). Similarly, the library will choose whether to purchase e-books using patron-driven models or evidence-based acquisition.

Open Access Literature

Open access literature is digital, online, free of charge, and free of most copyright and licensing restrictions (Suber 2012, 2). The figures for the overall prevalence of open access show that open access levels have increased steadily across all disciplines, from 20.4% of all scholarly outputs in 2008 to 23% in 2010 and more than one third of all scholarly outputs later than 2010 (Severin 2020, 5). Although the open access uptake in the humanities is lower than in most other fields, undeniably open access publications have become a focal point in the collection development of theological libraries. This trend will only increase in the coming years.

By selecting and making accessible these resources via catalog records and federated search tools, libraries are implicitly telling their patrons that the resources have met the library's standards of quality and relevance and are to be used alongside commercial, fee-based information resources. The provision of access via the library is a credentialing, deliberate function that has collection-related implications (Horava 2010, 144). Therefore, fundamental options with regard to systematically selecting, disclosing, and archiving open access content should be included in the collection development policy. As it does for purchased or licensed publications, the library selects or 'harvests' open access content in line with its collection profile. In this context, the collection development policy can play an important role in making agreements between large theological libraries about the systematic selection, effective dispensing, and sustainable preservation of open access content in line with their historically determined collection profiles. If the large libraries assume their role in this, it may have very beneficial effects on small or medium-sized libraries. As the mainstream collections become increasingly comprised of open access materials whose sustainable accessibility is assured by large libraries, small or medium-sized libraries can limit their collection building to complementary and specialized collections of books, journals, and databases needed by their users but not (yet) available in open access (cf. Kemp 2014, 389).

Deliberate decisions have to be made on the kind of open access items that are to be made available (e.g., only gold open access items with CC license) and which version is disclosed (e.g., only published version). The library must also decide whether to invest a part of the collection budget in strategically important open access projects, so that relevant open access collections are preserved and made accessible in a sustainable way. A library could, for instance, decide to put aside 2.5% of the total library budget to support open and community-owned infrastructure (Cf. Verbeke 2021).

Finally, decisions have to be made with regard to transformative agreements. Transformative agreements are publishing contracts that seek to transform the business model of scholarly publishing, namely to move from a subscription-based model where readers pay to read, to an open access model where writers pay to publish. These agreements represent a further shift away from a subscription-only model to one which covers both subscription payments (the "read" element of the agreement) and article processing charges (the "publish" element). Transformative agreements will require a substantial investment from academic institutions, as a kind of new form of big-deals packaging of scholarly communication (Verbeke, 2019). Therefore, caution is required and a well thought-out policy should be developed in this regard.

Finally, part of the open access policy of a library should concern its role in providing long-term access to institutional output (publications of staff, dissertations and research data, green open access materials) that can also be considered part of the collection.

Special and Legacy Collections

In the last decade, the value of special collections in the collection development policy of academic libraries has grown significantly. The reasons for this increased value are closely related to the breakthrough of a digital network environment. On the one hand, as electronic resources become increasingly available and the collections of large research libraries seem homogenized, special collections offer an opportunity to distinguish the identity of an academic library (Rossmann 2020, 633). A library that can make available online for research and education unique resources like rare books, manuscripts, or archives—clearly distinguishable from ubiquitous mainstream scholarly content—might set itself apart in attracting scholars and students (Clark 2014, 433). In a digital environment, these special collections undeniably become more and more iconic. More importantly, digitization and open licensing of digital cultural heritage has immensely increased access to special collections, bringing major benefits to research and education (Terras 2015). Whereas before digitization the use of special collections was mostly limited to the immediate community served by the library, access to this heritage content can now be opened up for the international scholarly community. The digitization of special collections has been an important step in facilitating theological research by providing convenient access to primary historical sources.

By 'legacy collections' is meant here "bibliographic items or collections which reflect that portion of a Library's holdings which is the result of former teaching, research and broader cultural collecting" (McCarthy 2007, 351). It is that part of the collection which is not rated either as special or highly functional and therefore not likely to be fully digitized in the long-term future.

With regard to special and heritage collections, the collection development policy should at least contain a policy regarding gifts and a policy regarding digitization and disclosure.

The acquisition of special and legacy collections is usually passive: they are donated by religious institutions or private persons. Not infrequently, these are extensive provenance collections, which therefore play an important role in the collection development of theological libraries, all the more so because the relevance of older publications remains high for historically oriented theological scholarship. Thus, theological libraries will often add offered collections to their collection and make them accessible as effectively as possible. Consequently, a collection development policy should include fundamental guidelines on, among other things, conditions for acceptance and criteria for deselection.

A collection development policy may also contain a plan of approach concerning the priorities to be set for digitizing special and legacy collections, the collection budget to be allocated, and the way in which the digitized content will be made available to the widest possible audience, taking into account copyright issues. This plan can turn these special and legacy collections of both large and smaller institutions into inside-out resources of the library collection and thereby provide an unique contribution to the development of the open access collection in the field of theology.

Conclusion

In the digital era, collection development policies should help us to address the fact that the former ideals of control, permanence, and relative exhaustivity in collection development have to be redefined. In a network environment, libraries are dependent on community-sourced solutions with regard to their basic functions of providing access to relevant content and preservation of this content for future generations, functions that were previously organized locally. What constitutes the library's collection is changing rapidly and thus its collection development strategy should be reprioritized. In order to continue to fulfill the library's role in collection development in an effective manner, many well-considered decisions are required regarding the selection of content, the choice of certain acquisition models, and the division of the collection budget between acquisition/licensing, investment in open infrastructure, and digitization. This increasing number of choices demands, among other things, an effective partnership between the library and the research community in the development of both collection and collection planning and collaboration with other libraries. Drawing up a collection development policy as an internal planning and decision-making tool and as a foundation for partnership and collaboration with external partners is therefore a valuable strategic objective.

Works Cited

American Library Association. 1979. "Guidelines for Collection Development." Chicago: American Library Association.

———. 1989. "Guide for Written Collection Policy Statements." Chicago: American Library Association.

———. 1996. "Guide for Written Collection Policy Statements." Chicago: American Library Association.

Andersen, Rick. 2011. "Collections 2021: The Future of the Library Collection Is Not a Collection." *Serials* 24, no. 3: 211–15.

Dempsey, Lorcan, Constance Malpas, and Brian Lavoie. 2014. "Collection Directions: The Evolution of Library Collections and Collecting." *Portal: Libraries and the Academy* 14, no. 3: 393–423.

Douglas, C. Steven. 2011. "Revisiting a Collection Development Policy in a Rapidly Changing Environment." *Journal of Electronic Resources in Medical Libraries* 8, no. 1: 15–21.

Horava, Tony. 2010. "Challenges and Possibilities for Collection Management in a Digital Age." *Library Resources & Technical Services* 54, no. 3: 142–52.

IFLA. 2001. "Guidelines for a Collection Development Policy Using the Conspectus Model." *https://repository.ifla.org/handle/123456789/52*.

Johnson, Peggy. 2009. *Fundamentals of Collection Development and Management*. Chicago: American Library Association.

Kempf, Klaus. 2014. "Bibliotheken ohne Bestand? Bestandsaufbau unter digitalen Vorzeichen." *Bibliothek, Forschung und Praxis* 38, no. 3: 365–97.

Levine-Clark, Michael. 2014. "Access to Everything: Building the Future Academic Library Collection." *Portal: Libraries and the Academy* 14, no. 3: 425–37.

McCarthy, J. P. 2007. "Some Thoughts on Legacy Collections." *Library Management* 28 no. 6/7: 347–54.

Pinfield, Stephen, Andrew Cox, and Sophie Rutter. 2017. "Mapping the Future of Academic Libraries. A Report for SCONUL." *https://sconul.ac.uk/sites/default/files/documents/Mapping%20the%20Future%20of%20Academic%20Libraries%20Final%20proof_0.pdf*.

Rossman, Jae Jennifer. 2020. "Investigating the Perceived Value of Special Collections in the Academic Library." *Journal of Library Administration* 60, no. 6: 631–44.

Severin, Anna, Matthias Egger, Martin Paul Eve, and Daniël Hürlimann. 2020. "Discipline-specific Open Access Publishing Practices and Barriers to Change: An Evidence-based Review." *F1000 Research 2020* 7: 1–42. *https://doi.org/10.12688/f1000research.17328.2*.

Suber, Peter. 2012. *Open Access*. Cambridge, MA: MIT. *https://openaccesseks.mitpress.mit.edu.*

Terras, Melissa. 2015. "Opening Access to Collections: The Making and Using of Open Digitised Cultural Content." *Online Information Review* 39, no. 5: 733–52.

Van Zijl, Carol. 1998. "The Why, What, and How of Collection Development Policies." *South African Journal of Libraries and Information Science* 66, no. 3: 99–106.

Verbeke, Demmy. 2019. "Safekeeping Diversity in Scholarly Communication: How 'Transformative' Are Recent Agreements"? *ScholarLed*, October 24. *https://blog.scholarled.org/safekeeping-diversity-in-scholarly-communication.*

———. 2021. "Not Only Transformative Agreements." *Scholarly Tales*, March 16. *https://scholarlytales.hcommons.org/2021/03/16/not-only-transformative-agreements.*

Vickery, Jim. 2004. "Making A Statement: Reviewing the Case for Written Collection Development Policies." *Library Management* 25, no. 8/9: 337–42.

CHAPTER 4

Constructing the Narrative

Best Practices in Resource Selection for Building Diverse, Equitable, and Inclusive Theological Collections

> *The high purpose of book selection is to provide the right book for the right reader at the right time.*
>
> – Francis K.W. Drury (1930, 1)

MARTA SAMOKISHYN

L IBRARY COLLECTIONS ARE CONSIDERED THE HEART OF THE UNIVERSITY (FIELD-house and Marshall 2012; Oakleaf 2010). They are one of the deciding factors for graduate students choosing an academic institution (Kallio 1995). In addition, research indicates that library collections help universities attract and retain researchers, increase research funding, and foster the value of scholarship and knowledge creation (Research Libraries UK and Research Information Network 2011; Tenopir, Volentine, and King 2012). Collection development librarians have an immense responsibility: to ensure that the collections they develop are relevant, current, and meet the needs of their users. A large part of this responsibility is based on the choice of a collection development librarian. Therefore, how we develop library collections is of utmost importance.

This is especially relevant when we consider the need to represent marginalized communities and their voices, which have not always been visible in our collections. Historically, many collections have represented the view of the dominant culture, or what some authors call the "culture of whiteness" (Brook, Ellenwood, and Lazzaro 2015, 247). As a result, the voices of underrepresented groups are not always included in the library collections. The diversity, equity, and inclusion framework (further DEI, also known as EDI, EDI-D) allows collection development librarians to "re-examine and re-calibrate their collection practices," especially taking into consideration increasingly diverse campuses (Estelle-Holmer, Limpitlaw, and Spomer 2021, 81). According to Cruz (2019, 220), "diversity is a cornerstone of the library profession." Bringing awareness of the diversity issues in academic libraries "provides tools for the social justice work" (Brook, Ellenwood, and Lazzaro 2015, 276). In addition, it is important for theological libraries to also acknowledge how they might have contributed to the current problem: "To truly embrace our social responsibility for promoting social justice, librarians and library leaders must also acknowledge the ways in which library practices frequently contribute to inequity, marginalization, and injustices; and commit to transforming our practices and standards in ways that leverage the power, expertise, and responsibility of academic librarians and libraries as forces for social justice" (Morales, Knowles, and Bourg 2014, 448).

To meet the needs of a diverse student population and faculty, as well as to ensure the effective use of library collections, it is vital to address this issue on the collection development level, including through collection development policies and strategies, and collection management, evaluation, and stewardship. Developing diversity plans or a diversity statement for the library can help formalize the commitment to DEI (Gujilde 2021; Herrera 2016). It must be done with particular focus and intentionality (Blume and Roylance 2020) since academic librarians have a duty to call attention to the underrepresented voices (Wagner and Crowley 2020): "Decolonizing academic library collections describes the work necessary to combat a traditionally Eurocentric focus by focusing on intentionally acquiring materials" (Blume and Roylance 2020, "Introduction").

This chapter, therefore, will address best practices in resource selection in theological libraries, with special attention given to selection strategies in small theological libraries, which often have limited resources and rely on internal and external partnerships to increase collection access and value. While small academic theological libraries are often at a disadvantage due to budget restrictions and possible space limitations, they provide a unique contribution to the community at large through their distinctive collections. Before diving into specific strategies, it is important to highlight several foundational approaches that can inform diversity and inclusion in collection development strategies. These approaches should be included in the collection development policies, even though they do not explicitly use DEI language.

Foundational Approaches for the Adoption of DEI Practices in Collection Development

Before we proceed, it is essential to define DEI in the context of collection development (Ciszek and Young 2010). A DEI framework covers a broad social justice approach to collection development that has diversity, equity, and inclusion as its central foundational values. It "consider[s] and affirm[s] the role of multiple identities with relationship to various social contexts and interlocking systems of power, privilege, and oppression" (Özturgut 2017, 87). Here are the definitions of diversity, equity, and inclusion, according to the Social Sciences and Humanities Research Council of Canada (SSHRC):

> a) Diversity is "differences in race, colour, place of origin, religion, immigrant and newcomer status, ethnic origin, ability, sex, sexual orientation, gender identity, gender expression and age";
> b) Equity is "the removal of systemic barriers and biases enabling all individuals to have equal opportunity to access and benefit from the program";
> c) Inclusion is "the practice of ensuring that all individuals are valued and respected for their contributions and are equally supported" (2021, under "What is 'EDI'?").

See a list of recommended resources on topics related to DEI at *atla. libguides.com/DEI*.

Even though the DEI framework has not been widely discussed in the LIS literature on collection development, we can apply these principles to the way we develop our library collections. Thus, when it comes to collection development, DEI means building library collections with the consistent consideration of multiple voices from the community, taking into account race, colour, ethnic origin, immigration status, social status, theological views, sex, sexual orientation, gender expression, age, and physical and learning abilities, etc., by providing equitable access and representation of these voices in order to include users' needs as the focal point of the collection. In addition, DEI-informed collections should draw on different theological traditions and the lived experience of people and groups from different faith backgrounds, with particular attention to global issues (Estelle-Holmer, Limpitlaw, and Spomer 2021). Integration of DEI practices, in turn, will further encourage exploration of the DEI-related topics in the local communities of inquiry. Several essential factors or foundational approaches that can help us adopt DEI practices in our collection development strategies include curriculum alignment, a user-centred approach to collection development, and community engagement.

Curriculum Alignment

Curriculum alignment is often a central piece of collection development policies. It allows librarians responsible for collections to identify new programs, create a plan for existing programs and research centres, and ensure the collection they are building meets the needs of all the programs offered by the institution. The degree levels of new and existing programs are essential considerations, since graduate programs require advanced academic resources to meet the needs of their students and researchers. Curriculum alignment can help us identify relevant DEI themes for each program, including but not limited to the following: BIPOC (Black, Indigenous, and people of colour) theology, eco-theology, LGBTQIA2+ issues, Indigenous approaches to theology, theology of disabled bodies, etc. Curriculum alignment can serve as a guide to help us think about important DEI issues and identify areas of a collection that are multidisciplinary and multifaceted. To facilitate curriculum alignment with the DEI principles in mind, please see table 1.

Table 1 — Curriculum Alignment Matrix

Faculty	Dept./ Prog.	Prog. levels	DEI topics	Major book publishers	Major journals	Major series
e.g., Theology	e.g., Pastoral theology	e.g., DMin, MDiv	e.g., BIPOC authors	e.g., Wipf & Stock	e.g., *Liberation Theology*	e.g., African Theo. Studies

User-centered Approach to Collection Development

"Libraries exist for their users" (Nixon, Freeman, and Ward 2011, 1). Anticipating the needs of current and future library users is one of the most important tasks of a librarian responsible for collections. It requires being in sync with the existing library patrons and understanding and anticipating their needs. This task can be quite difficult because we, as librarians, "often serve a large and diverse community of users" (Agee 2007, 1). As Agee points out, "to have a collection of value to library users, it is necessary to know who those users are." It is less challenging in small academic libraries because it is easier to know students by name and know their research interests. Attending research seminars to hear students' presentations on their doctoral or master's thesis proposals is one helpful strategy to adopt a user-centered approach to collection development. In addition, if a librarian who does collection development also is involved in information literacy instruction and reference, they have additional opportunities to get to know students and their topics of inquiry.

Liaison with the faculty members is crucial to understanding library users' unique characteristics—including faculty and student cultural backgrounds, theological traditions, demographics, research interests, research projects, and more—which in turn can help facilitate DEI-informed collections. Users, thus, drive the diversity of the collections.

To know library users, many librarians create community analysis studies, including surveys, focus groups, interviews, etc. These methods can help identify and better understand the needs of the underrepresented library users and adjust library collection strategies accordingly. Statistics provided by the university or college administration can help establish the percentage of students with disability, international students, or those students who identify as BIPOC and/ or LGTBQIA2+. While the acquisition of the materials related to DEI should not depend on the statistical data, its analysis can help to connect to the community of local library users and encourage budget allocation to specific themes. According to Gujilde (2021), this creates a stronger sense of belonging among the members of academic communities and libraries.

Here is an example of a tool that can be used to understand library users when it comes to DEI (table 2). It presents a non-exhaustive list that can help establish some general considerations for community analysis and understanding how users' needs can be met.

However, it is also important to highlight that DEI-related material is relevant not only to the populations it seeks to represent but to the entire student body and faculty. It "prepare[s] students for their entry into the real world" (Vega García 2000, 319).

Table 2 — Understanding Library Users: Community Analysis (adapted from Agee 2007)

Population groups (Who)	Resources consideration (What)
BIPOC users	Acquisition of resources by BIPOC authors and/or related to BIPOC theological themes
Non-native English speakers	Bilingual or foreign-language resources
Users with disability	Large print books, availability of oral readers and other technologies
LGBTQIA2+ users	Acquisition of resources by LGBTQIA2+ authors and/or related to LGBTQIA2+ themes;

Community Engagement Strategies

The main objective of academic library collections is to "meet the information needs of local library users" (Agee 2007, 1). While maintaining this focus on the local library community of students, faculty, and other researchers, it is also important to create partnerships with external communities that might advocate and support DEI-related issues outside campuses, such as research institutes, non-profit organizations, and other partner institutions. Establishing liaison with the community at large can help foster potential library donations (discussed below) as well as help determine how the library can serve members of said community.

Now that we have touched on several foundational approaches to adapt DEI-informed practices to collection development, I would like to discuss specific strategies used by librarians to make their library collections more diverse, equitable, and inclusive.

Collection Development Strategies

Collection development strategies are constantly evolving as new technologies and products become available. The strategies discussed below can be applied to developing monograph collections, which constitutes 80–90% of collection development decisions. These strategies can be adapted to the context of the specific library, taking into account its size, budget, subject coverage, student and faculty population, and the community at large. Table 3 (over) focuses on different components of collection development thought processes, assumptions, and solutions related to DEI.

According to Johnson (2004), experience and intuition play an important role in selecting resources. However, knowing specific tools and collection development strategies is essential for success. In addition, Young (2006) states that librarians need to be equipped with tools and methods to track the diversity of their acquisitions.

Recommendations by Faculty and Students

Recommendations made by faculty and students are an essential part of overall collection development strategies. Indeed, recommendations are vital because they ensure that the collection remains relevant to the users. Some faculty members are committed to recommending resources in their field on a regular basis. This should be encouraged because some faculty and students might feel uncomfortable asking a librarian to spend part of their library bud-

Table 3 — DEI in Collection Development (inspired by Sullivan 2020)

Aspect of collection development	False assumptions	Impacts	Solution
DEI-related content (BIPOC theo., eco-theology, LGTBQIA2+ issues, theo. of disabled bodies, etc.)	• If my institution does not have diverse population groups, I do not need to purchase DEI-related content. • There are no researchers in my institution who work on these topics; therefore, I do not need to purchase DEI-related content.	• Strong disconnect and no sense of belonging among library users. • No historical record for future researchers & students about theological issues related to DEI. • Significant gaps in the collection.	• Creating a stronger sense of community and belonging among library users. • Comprehensive collection without significant topical gaps.
Format (print, electronic)	• Everyone always prefers only one format (either print or electronic). • Because my institution does not offer distance programs, I don't require resources in electronic format.	• Limited access to the print collection for groups who are unable to come and study on campus (single parents, people with disability, etc.). • Technology barriers for electronic access.	• Identifying the needs of different groups. • Creating alternative programs for people who have tech-related barriers to access. • Purchasing multiple formats for core resources.

Table 3 — DEI in Collection Development (inspired by Sullivan 2020)

Aspect of collection development	False assumptions	Impacts	Solution
Languages	· Collection development in other languages is unnecessary. · Not many people in my institution currently speak other languages.	· Monoculturalism. · Lack of culturally diverse collections.	· Incorporating culturally diverse resources in other languages. · Identifying core resources for theology in other languages based on programs of study & focus.
Content level	· There is no place for popular sources in an academic library. · All students should be using the same content-level sources in their studies.	· Lack of denominational "popular" sources can make collection irrelevant for students in pastoral ministry. · Students of different cognitive abilities can feel overwhelmed by the lack of diversity in content level.	· Ensure the needs of students who work in pastoral ministry or pastoral theology are met by ordering "popular" religious content when applicable. · Create equitable collections with varied content levels, incl. general & adv. academic literature, to meet needs of students of different abilities.

get on resources for their research. It is crucial, however, to consider that faculty recommendations are usually not done systematically throughout the institution (Whipple 2006). This can result in uneven collections, which might require additional intervention as well as the development of a systematic process for faculty input to ensure equal representation of all voices across the collection. It can take the form of a communication plan between liaison/collection development librarians and the faculty members or of an ongoing communication to help faculty review collections in their research areas and make recommendations to fill any gaps they have identified in the collection.

Syllabi

USING COURSE SYLLABI TO IDENTIFY CORE TEXTS FOR EACH COURSE IS AN ESSENTIAL TOOL and strategy for collection development. This can further ensure that all course-recommended readings are equally represented in the library collection and that the library provides students with equitable access to these core texts.

Selection through Automated Acquisition Providers

EBSCO's GOBI acquisition platform is one of the most widely used providers of library resources in North America. Other vendors include Midwest Library Service, Coutts Library Services, Harrassowitz, etc. Using providers' platforms allows librarians to have convenient and easy access to many publishers and subjects as well as a practical, hands-on method for ordering resources. It also provides the ability to set up approval plans, which might be somewhat challenging to small academic libraries with budget limitations. When setting a library profile with a library provider, a librarian will consider classification ranges for the subject parameters represented in the curriculum. In addition, it is important to consider non-subject parameters that may include many DEI-inspired criteria, such as different languages, content level (popular, basic studies, general academic, advanced academic, professional), place of publication, non-book format, topical aspects (e.g., religion, social work), and interdisciplinary topics (e.g., Black studies, Hispanic studies, gerontology, LGBTQIA2+ studies, Indigenous studies, women's studies). These interdisciplinary topics in the ordering profiles are essential to consider. In addition, it is important to have a list of publishers for the library's ordering profile. Including smaller theological publishers that focus on specific DEI-related themes can increase the visibility of these themes in the collection and diversify it so that it encompasses a variety of voices.

Periodical Lists / Book Reviews / Publishers' Catalogues

Additional layers of collection development strategies can come from periodical lists, book reviews, and publishers' catalogues. While automated acquisition platforms provide a comprehensive picture of new publications and are very convenient to use, they might not always be enough. In some cases, when the resource is produced by small presses, religious communities, or other independent publishers, or when the book is self-published, it might not be included in the automated platform. Thus, for example, some publishers important to consider for literature on pastoral ministry are: Novalis, Westminster John Knox, Fortress Press, Eerdmans, InterVarsity Press (IVP), among others. Furthermore, some subject areas, such as canon law, require special collection development strategies due to their specificity and unique content. In these cases, reviewing the most recent periodical issues to find the "Books received" section can be beneficial. It will often contain a list of books related to the topic of a periodical issue, identify new publications, and provide book reviews. Additional book reviews from sources like *Review of Biblical Literature, Religious Studies Review, Theologische Literaturzeitung,* and *Revue d'histoire ecclésiastique* can help make a decision. However, reading book reviews is often a time-consuming task and may not always be feasible. In addition, by the time book reviews appear, a significant amount of time has passed. Consequently, it is also helpful to check Amazon lists for theology (sorting by date of publication) and publishers' catalogues (print or online). Roy (2017) also suggests following publishers and award-winning authors on social media for announcements of new publications. Meeting publishers at conferences, such as Atla Annual, can help librarians enlarge the librarian's circle of small publishers and help the library learn about their new titles. Although libraries can request catalogues from publishers to review them for new titles, this practice should only serve as a supplementary strategy since subject-based selection through periodical lists and service-providers, like GOBI, can provide better subject coverage.

It is important to highlight, as Little (2013) points out, that many small presses, including religious community publishers in ministry and pastoral theology, will be affiliated with a certain denomination. They can be considered "biased" towards one denomination; however, as Little states, these sources "capture contemporary Christian thought and practice, and reveal contemporary attitudes towards important social questions" (119), and are therefore important for theological collections. They also provide a unique character for local collections and can benefit collaboration between institutions from different faith traditions.

Approval Plans and Standing Orders

When it comes to placing orders on platforms like GOBI, large academic libraries often rely on approval plans—automatic purchases of monographs based on the criteria specified by a librarian, such as subject areas, publishers, publication format, languages, and more. Approval plans can help librarians save time, especially if they are committed to building comprehensive collections in specific subject areas. They can also be a convenient way to add DEI-related topics to their collections. Due to budget limitations, small academic libraries do not normally rely on approval plans. However, standing orders for monographic series can help librarians save time on the selection process and ensure orders are coming in continuously while the librarian locates harder-to-find materials. Reference works can be part of standing orders, especially in the case of multi-volume works. Special attention needs to be paid to Bible dictionaries, encyclopaedias, handbooks, concordances, Bible commentaries in different faith traditions, and language dictionaries (including Hebrew, Latin, and Classical Greek).

Selection of Resources by Specific Criteria

Language

Libraries will often collect resources in other languages, especially if they have a bilingual student population or if their institution offers advanced degrees in theology. As a librarian from a bilingual university in Canada, I have to acknowledge that collecting for a bilingual institution can sometimes be challenging, especially taking into account the lack of resources in specific areas in some languages. Very often, francophone students who do not speak English are not able to translate material for themselves and require additional support with locating sources. In addition, it is important to consider which programs are unilingual and which programs are bilingual within the university to provide adequate support. It is also important to ensure that budget is allocated accordingly when taking into account the language of the resource. Many institutions with advanced degrees in theology develop collections in such European languages as French, German, Italian, Greek, and Spanish. This helps to ensure that important works in theology from other continents are accessible. Some institutions also develop special collections in Indigeneous languages to preserve the resources of specific Indigenous peoples. Thus, for example, the library of Saint Paul University collects and preserves resources in various Indigenous languages, including Cree, Slave, Anishinini, Dene, Inuktitut, as well as a few others. The collection includes two manuscript dictionaries: one Cree-French and the other Slave-French, both complied by Oblate missionaries. Other works in the collection in Indigenous languages include missals, prayer books, grammar manuals, etc.

The challenge of collecting in other languages is often related to the language expertise of the collection development librarian. This can be addressed through internal and external partnerships. Thus, for example, Saint Paul University Library partners with the Indigenous center on campus. In addition, some professors might be willing to help with the languages as well, especially when it comes to languages that do not use the Latin alphabet (such as Arabic, Cyrillic, Georgian, or Greek).

Format (print/electronic)

Deciding on the format of a resource requires careful consideration of the user demographics. Due to the COVID-19 pandemic, many libraries have switched to acquiring material in electronic format when possible. This, however, comes with a cost, since unlimited licences for e-books are usually three to five times more expensive than paper copies. Nevertheless, the electronic format can provide more equitable access to students and faculty, especially when taking distance students into consideration. But it is also essential to recognize and acknowledge that electronic content might be limited in some disciplines.

ILLs and Other Borrowing Requests

Interlibrary loans (ILLs) and other borrowing request data (e.g., requests made in the discovery layer tool) can be an important tool for collection development. Analysis of ILL requests can inform a collection development librarian of the gaps in the collection. It is crucial to look for systematic gaps related to DEI themes. While other strategies focus on the "just-in-case" acquisition mode, this strategy can be characterized as a "just-in-time" inventory model (Nixon, Freeman, and Ward 2011). If the budget allows, this strategy can be used to fill those gaps and reflect on whether collection development should be adjusted in the future. However, if a library has a limited budget, relying on ILLs and other borrowing opportunities is beneficial, especially for out-of-print resources or resources in other languages.

Evaluation of Collection Use by Library Users

Reviewing borrowing data for both print and electronic resources can indicate how the users are using the collection, what resources are being circulated, and how these trends can further inform the collection development decisions.

Adding Open Access Books and Journals to the Collection

Adding open access books (such as the ones published by Atla Open Press) and open access journals can enrich library collections by making these resources visible to diverse users in the library catalogue. See, for example, the Open Access Digital Theological Library (*oadtl.org/open-access-journals*) and Directory of Open Access Journals (*doaj.org*).

Donations

Donations can be an important tool for growing a library collection, especially when the library budget is limited and there is a high need to fill the gaps in the collection. Specific donations can also provide critical DEI-related materials and help diversify the collection since donors usually offer subject-based donations. However, it is important to remember that donations also require additional human and financial resources for sorting, checking, and cataloguing. In addition, institutions provide certain kinds of tax receipts for donations, when applicable. In the US, libraries cannot assign a value to a donation. Donations that are not accepted can be redistributed to students or sent to organizations such as Better World Books.

Cross-checking with Other Local Collections and Consortia

Local library communities can be an essential resource for library users if a library has budget limitations. Small academic libraries, especially, can rely on community partnerships. Before purchasing a resource, it can be beneficial to check if other local libraries already own it. However, this strategy has its limitations: inconvenience to the users, potential gaps in the collections, and possible future weeding of those materials that are beyond our control.

Special Considerations for Selecting Databases and Periodicals

New periodicals and databases can provide enormous value to library users. Faculty often recommend journals for subscriptions. Reviewing faculty publications can also inform the decision about journal subscriptions. To stay on top of new journal titles, it is important to check existing database indexes, the Directory of Open Access Journals, and publishers' announcements. Subscribing to the vendors' email lists is another way to receive news about new journals or databases. Requesting trials for databases can provide use data to help a librarian decide whether there is interest from library users.

Conclusion

This chapter has provided an overview of some collection development strategies that libraries can use to diversify their collections. It is important to note that these strategies can be applied to building current collections as well as filling the DEI-related gaps in the existing collections (Bowers, Crowe, and Keeran 2017). For retrospective collection development, such providers as AbeBooks, Alibris, or Better World Books can be helpful.

As Carrigan (1988, 22) stated, "the essence of collection development is choice." This makes the job of a collection development librarian unique because with every choice comes power and responsibility. It is the power to construct the narrative of your library and an impact "on who and what is represented in the scholarly and cultural record" (Morales, Knowles, and Bourg 2014, 445–46). The same power to make decisions about what resources to order that was often used to censor specific topics in the past can now increase the visibility of marginalized voices and communities.

Collection development does not happen in a vacuum (Uplaonkar and Kalikadevi, 2018). Librarians have to ensure that "their personal experiences, perspectives, and biases do not consciously or unconsciously influence" (Johnson 2004, 127) their decision to include or exclude certain themes from the collections. Collection development librarians "must approach collection development from a certain personal and emotional distance and employ analytical skills and sound judgement" (Little 2013, 123). This is a responsibility to all current and future library users who will rely on these collections to tell their stories, inquire about their past, and contribute to scholarship in their field of study. Through diverse collections, the readers can experience a more profound sense of belonging and connection. Therefore, library collections require a holistic vision to create usable library collections. Including multiple voices and perspectives in the collection ensures that diverse, equitable, and inclusive collections will meet the needs of all the library stakeholders and can remain sustainable for future users. This is the responsible stewardship to which we as theological librarians are called. Being open to the "creative potential of difference" can help librarians not only to transform library collections, but also to "transform academic libraries" as a whole (Brook, Ellenwood, and Lazzaro 2015, 277).

Works Cited

Agee, Jim. 2007. *Acquisitions Go Global: An Introduction to Library Collection Management in the 21st Century.* Oxford: Chandos.

Blume, Rachel, and Allyson Roylance. 2020. "Decolonization in Collection Development: Developing an Authentic Authorship Workflow." *Journal of Academic Librarianship* 46, no. 5. *https:// doi.org/10.1016/j.acalib.2020.102175.*

Bowers, Jennifer, Katherine Crowe, and Peggy Keeran. 2017. "'If You Want the History of a White Man, You Go to the Library': Critiquing Our Legacy, Addressing Our Library Collections Gaps." *Collection Management* 42, nos. 3–4: 159–79. *https://doi.org/10.108 0/01462679.2017.1329104.*

Brook, Freeda, Dave Ellenwood, and Althea Eannace Lazzaro. 2015. "In Pursuit of Antiracist Social Justice: Denaturalizing Whiteness in the Academic Library." *Library Trends* 64, no. 2: 246–84. *https://doi.org/10.1353/lib.2015.0048.*

Carrigan, Dennis P. 1988. "Librarians and the 'Dismal Science.'" *Library Journal* 113, no. 11): 22–25.

Ciszek, Matthew P., and Courtney L. Young. 2010. "Diversity Collection Assessment in Large Academic Libraries." *Collection Building* 29, no. 4: 154–61. *https://doi.org/10.1108/01604951011088899.*

Cruz, Alice M. 2019. "Intentional Integration of Diversity Ideals in Academic Libraries: A Literature Review." *Journal of Academic Librarianship* 45, no. 3: 220–27. *https://doi.org/10.1016/j.acalib.2019.02.011.*

Drury, Francis, K. W. 1930. *Book Selection.* Chicago: American Library Association.

Estelle-Holmer, Suzanne, Amy Limpitlaw, and Michelle Spomer. 2021. "Can You Find Yourself in the Stacks? Building Diverse Collections in Religion and Theology." In *Atla Summary of Proceedings* 75, 81–116. *https://serials.atla.com/proceedings/issue/view/251/201.*

Fieldhouse, Margaret, and Audrey Marshall. 2012. *Collection Development in the Digital Age*. London: Facet Publishing.

Gujilde, Paolo P. 2021. "Moving Beyond Buzzwords: Belonging in Library Collections." In *Hope and a Future: Perspectives on the Impact that Librarians and Libraries Have on Our World*, edited by Renee F. Hill, 35–41. Bingley: Emerald. *https://emerald.com/insight/content/doi/10.1108/S0065-283020210000048004/full/html*.

Herrera, Gail. 2016. "Undergraduate Library Collection Use and Diversity: Testing for Racial and Gender Differences." *Portal: Libraries and the Academy* 16, no. 4: 763–74. *https://doi.org/10.1353/pla.2016.0051*.

Johnson, Peggy. 2004. *Fundamentals of Collection Development & Management*. Chicago: American Library Association.

Kallio, Ruth E. 1995. "Factors Influencing the College Choice Decisions of Graduate Students." *Research in Higher Education* 36, no. 1: 109–24. *https://doi.org/10.1007/BF02207769*.

Little, Geoffrey. 2013. "Collection Development for Theological Education." In *Library Collection Development for Professional Programs: Trends and Best Practices*, edited by Sara Holder, 112–27. Hershey, PA: IGI Global. *https://doi.org./10.4018/978-1-4666-1897-8.ch007*.

Morales, Myrna, Em Claire Knowles, and Chris Bourg. 2014. "Diversity, Social Justice, and the Future of Libraries." *Portal: Libraries and the Academy* 14, no. 3): 439–51. *https://doi.org/10.1353/pla.2014.0017*.

Nixon, Judith M., Robert S. Freeman, and Suzanne M. Ward. 2011. *Patron-Driven Acquisitions: Current Successes and Future Directions*. London: Routledge.

Oakleaf, Megan. 2010. *The Value of Academic Libraries: A Comprehensive Research Review and Report*. Chicago: Association of College and Research Libraries.

Özturgut, Osman. 2017. "Internationalization for Diversity, Equity, and Inclusion." *Journal of Higher Education Theory and Practice* 17, no. 6: 83–91. *https://na-businesspress.com/JHETP/OzturgutO_17_6_.pdf*.

Research Libraries UK and Research Information Network. 2011. *The Value of Libraries for Research and Researchers: A RIN and*

RLUK Report. https://rluk.ac.uk/wp-content/uploads/2014/02/Value-of-Libraries-report.pdf.

Roy, Loriene. 2017. "Keeping Up: Building Your Indigenous Collection." *Collection Management* 42, nos. 3–4: 226–39. *https://doi.org/10.1080/01462679.2017.1328323.*

Social Sciences and Humanities Research Council. 2021. "Best Practices in Equity, Diversity and Inclusion in Research." New Frontiers in Research Fund. *https://sshrc-crsh.gc.ca/funding-financement/nfrf-fnfr/edi-eng.aspx#2.*

Tenopir, Carol, Rachel Volentine, and Donald W. King. 2012. "Scholarly Reading and the Value of Academic Library Collections: Results of a Study in Six UK Universities." *Insights* 25, no. 2: 130–49. *https://doi.org/10.1629/2048-7754.25.2.130.*

Uplaonkar, Shilpa, and Badiger G. Kalikadevi. 2018. "Strategies for Collection Development in Academic Libraries." *International Journal of Library and Information Studies* 8, no. 1: 149–54. *https://ijlis.org/articles/strategies-for-collection-development-in-academic-libraries.pdf.*

Vega García, Susan A. 2000. "Racial and Ethnic Diversity in Academic Library Collections: Ownership and Access of African American and U.S. Latino Periodical Literature." *Journal of Academic Librarianship* 26, no. 5): 311–22.

Wagner, Travis L., and Archie Crowley. 2020. "Why Are Bathrooms Inclusive If the Stacks Exclude? Systemic Exclusion of Trans and Gender Nonconforming Persons in Post-Trump Academic Librarianship." *Reference Services Review* 48, no. 1: 159–81. *https://doi.org/10.1108/RSR-10-2019-0072.*

Whipple, Caroline. 2006. "Collection Development in a Theological Research Library." In *A Broadening Conversation: Classic Readings in Theological Librarianship,* edited by Melody Layton McMahon and David R. Stewart, 99–105. Lanham, MD: Scarecrow Press. *https://doi.org/10.31046/atlapress.27.*

Young, Courtney L. 2006. "Collection Development and Diversity on CIC Academic Library Web Sites." *Journal of Academic Librarianship* 32, no. 4: 370–76. *https://doi.org/10.1016/j.acalib.2006.03.004.*

CHAPTER 5

Diversity, Equity, Inclusion, and Anti-racism in Collection Development

> *"Cultural Diversity" or "Multiculturalism" refers to the harmonious co-existence and interaction of different cultures, where "culture should be regarded as the set of distinctive spiritual, material, intellectual and emotional features of society or a social group, and that it encompasses, in addition to art and literature; lifestyles, ways of living together, value systems, traditions and beliefs.*
>
> – IFLA/UNESCO Multicultural Library Manifesto, 2012

ANITA COLEMAN

B Y POINTING OUT GLOBAL FORCES, SUCH AS 6,000 LANGUAGES IN THE WORLD, increasing international migration rates that result in complex identities, globalization, faster communication, ease of transportation, and other forces, the 2012 IFLA/UNESCO Multicultural Library Manifesto encourages the building of multicultural libraries. The manifesto's first two core actions (there's a total of five) to "develop culturally and linguistically diverse collections, including digital and multimedia resources; allocate resources for the preservation of cultural expression and heritage, paying particular attention to oral, indigenous and intangible cultural heritage" are based on the 2005 UNESCO Convention on the Protection and Promotion of the Diversity of Cultural Expressions. The 2005 Convention was a milestone in international cultural policy. Ratified by 150 UN member states, it affirms diversity as the heart of the creative economy. The cultural sector is now one of the fastest growing areas, making up 6.1% of the global economy, powering over 30 million jobs, and with an estimated global worth of $4.3 billion. The manifesto also includes a short guide for how individual libraries can participate.

The literature on libraries is filled with calls to build multicultural collections, but barriers exist. Globally, the digital divide, inequitable flows of information between countries, lack of trained staff, and funding are some of the challenges which the North American and Euro-centric discourse about diversity, equity, inclusion (DEI) and anti-racism often exacerbates. To ease some of these barriers, in this chapter definitions of DEI and anti-racism are first presented from an international perspective and then discussed with examples and best practices for library collection development. The goal is to empower librarians in low- and middle-income countries (LMICs) to identify priorities and develop best practices that would preserve local, Indigenous, and marginalized voices and make them more globally visible. Librarians everywhere will find it instructive.

Definitions

Definitions are adapted from the Anti-racism Digital Library (2022), which has a glossary of over 200 terms.

- Diversity encompasses different properties or characteristics that make one individual or group different from another.

- Equity is about dividing resources proportionally to achieve a fair outcome. Equity recognizes the important role played by the past in human capabilities and achievements in the present and for the future and seeks to address them fairly.

- Inclusion engages the community with practices that create an environment of belonging. It is best understood when juxtaposed against its opposite, exclusion. Inclusion, like anti-racism, creates belonging; exclusion creates othering.

- Anti-racism is focused and sustained action, by a mix of people which includes inter-cultural, inter-faith, multi-lingual and inter-abled communities with the intent to change a system or an institutional policy, practice, or procedure which has oppressive effects.

21st-century Collection Development: Think Globally, Act Locally

Authority, appropriateness, accuracy or timeliness, physical characteristics, collection fit, information quality, demand, content, and special characteristics are how information resources have generally been added to a library collection (Engelson 2015). DEI and anti-racism emerged towards the end of the 20th century (ALA; IFLA/UNESCO 2012).

There are many ways to incorporate DEI using the principle of "think globally, act locally." One of them is by being aware of gender inclusivity and equity in the local context, making inclusion an explicit policy criterion in library collection policies (Mbambo-Thata et al. 2019). Library user groups, especially women, the poor, Indigenous persons, and the historically under-represented, can be identified and named using local thesauri and in consultation with users. The library should strive to collect materials by these groups of authors, not merely provide resources for them as users. The key is to identify the marginalized, excluded people. For example, the Australian Institute of Aboriginal and Torres Strait Islanders (AIATSIS) has produced *Pathways*, a web gateway to thesauri for the collections of Indigenous languages and people (AIATSIS, 2021). If the community of users isn't yet fully understood and no thesaurus is available, browse the Atla Thesaurus of Religious Occupational Terms, Library of Congress Demographic Group Terms, and similar resources. Another way is to use the collection levels stated in the library's policy—in the US context: out of scope, minimal, basic information, instructional support, research, and comprehensive levels—and make exceptions inclusive. For example, because children's books are out of scope in a seminary library's collection development policy, a faculty member is using their own special collection developed over years. The library does not want to absorb the collection, but it names the "user groups" of this collection in its collection policy. With the cooperation of the faculty member, the library does a diversity audit of the collection to ensure that it is inclusive.

Types of diversity can help set collecting priorities. Some examples are:

1. **Cultural / historical diversity**, such as Indigenous knowledge held in oral histories, beliefs, and intangible cultural heritage. Indigenous knowledge (IK), historically marginalized and traditionally not collected by libraries, has been shown to be vital to the development of societies, nations, and economies. IK is often endangered because it is linked to linguistic diversity, collectively owned, and lacks documentation. Abioye and Oluwaniyi (2017) provide an excellent definition of library collection development as "the means of meeting the information needs of the people (a service population) in a timely and economical manner using information resources locally held, as well as from other organizations." They found that Nigerian federal libraries are engaged in IK collection development and preservation despite a lack of funding partners and bilingual librarians.

2. **Linguistic diversity,** such as dead or dying languages represented by patrons. Librarians should prioritize resources in the language of the users. Be informed about language hotspots, i.e., areas of the world with many languages near extinction (Living Tongues Institute for Endangered Languages 2022). Libraries in these regions (and those elsewhere with these people) can prioritize their documentation (texts, lexicons, dictionaries, A/V materials).

3. **Access diversity**, such as open access, open educational resources, and theological commons. The open access movement has gained ground, but the global south has become disillusioned by exorbitant article processing charges. Open access also lacks author geographic diversity (Smith et al. 2020). Plus, there's been little work done to integrate open access workflows and products into collection development (Dyas-Correaia and Devakos, 2014). Librarians must grasp these nuances. Librarians in the global north must reach out to those in the LMICs, who, however inadequate and inter-

mittent their digital access may be now, can form alliances that enrich the geographic and format diversity of open access. At a more prosaic level, Atla Digital Library, OAPEN, and Patheos all provide open access content in religion.

4. **Source diversity**, that is, materials are acquired from multiple sources. Outsourced collection development is rejected or managed stringently so that local selection can take advantage of local presses and alternative publishers who challenge mainstream views.

5. **Religious diversity**, including ecumenism, interfaith, and multi-faith studies, as well as folk religions. Christianity has emerged through several periods which can be broadly classified as classical, historical, ecumenical, and the present period of global consciousness. In this period of global consciousness, Christianity in the two-thirds world (also called the global south) is more dominant than in Europe-America and has relationships with other world religions (Center for the Study of Global Christianity, 2022). Folk religions and interspirituality are also increasing.

6. **Identity diversity**, such as users' experiential differences, neurodiversity, and professional diversity. An awareness of the special characteristics of users will help the librarian meet user needs. For example, learn from Charlie Remy, an academic librarian with autism (Remy 2018).

7. **Intellectual diversity** beyond conventional representation, experience, and points of view. Often "own voices" are missing in libraries. For example, the Circle of Concerned Woman African Theologians began publishing because, as Africans, women, and theologians in a male-centered, Western-dominated field they just could not find space for their voices to be heard. In the US, WNDB, a successful non-profit that is improving children's literature, started in 2014 from a tweet with the hashtag #WeNeedDiverseBooks bemoaning the lack of diversity in that field. Representation and "own voices" authorship, as well as materials citing "others" who are not often cited are critical for intellectual diversity.

8. **Format diversity**, such as audio-visual books, movies, e-books, and online content. Book industry reports show that audio books and e-books have increased in readership globally. The proliferation of digital videos and photos has outpaced the abilities of libraries to collect them. The spirituality and religion collection in the Moving Image Archive of the Internet Archive has 120,881 movies; within this is a sub-collection of Islamic Sermons and Lessons, which comprises 160,875 audio files and 40,814 movies. In light of the serials price crisis and declining book acquisitions, open access digital content first and rightsizing have become collection management priorities (Johnson 2012; Miller and Ward 2022). Titles of local and regional significance and titles not often held by others are preferred; participation in consortia and collaborative activities are employed to meet users' needs for less used materials. Saving Ukrainian Cultural Heritage Online is a dramatic example of how people and organizations came together to archive Ukrainian libraries' online content when Russia invaded Ukraine. The library's location in a conflict zone should also determine priorities.

Equity-informed Preparatory Practices for Collection Development

1. **Global South Publishing and Decolonization** — Reflect on the information divide inequities between the countries of the world and how collection development can support the de-northernization of the publishing landscape. De-northernization means breaking the many barriers to publishing in LMICs. It also includes decolonization, which simply means "decentering whiteness" in academic discourse (Cooke 2020). The Circle of Concerned African Women Theologians, established by Mercy Amba Oduyoye, was a result of both her own inspiration and the solidarity of Constance Buchanan at Harvard University. Oduyoye encouraged African women theologians to become members of the Ecumenical Association of Third World Theologians. Buchanan created a space for African women theologians to spend a year at Harvard

researching and writing (Labeodan 2016). Their voices were heard, their writings collected and read. This is an example of equity on a global level. Another example is the Library of Congress and Book Dash (South Africa) partnership to publish open access born-digital children's books (Darby 2019). Librarians must reclaim their ancient role in publishing.

2. **Unconscious Bias Training** — "Before engaging in any diversity audit planning, librarians should not only educate themselves about libraries, literature, and representation, but also reflect upon their own biases and attitudes" (Carmack 2021). Resource selection must begin with critical self-awareness. All humans have biases, many learned (Zecker 2013). This is nothing to be ashamed of. Unconscious (hidden) bias can be measured by implicit association tests and corrected with lifelong learning. A continuing education program of unconscious bias training and cultural competencies for staff and key stakeholders is highly recommended.

3. **Prioritization** — Prioritization of a subject area is key before beginning a diversity audit of the current collection and reviewing its policy. Actions will differ in various libraries but thinking globally, acting locally for incorporating DEI and anti-racism still helps. For example, a library near a language hotspot with uncollected Indigenous knowledge could choose IK and language diversity collection priorities and strive for digital open access. Conversely, anti-racism may not be a priority in countries which do not classify people by racial categories but rather collect ethnocultural data—ethnicity (ancestry or ethnic origin, nationality, Indigenous/Aboriginal groups, tribe or caste), language, and religion. In each of these examples, resources will be preferred that represent and are created by the historically marginalized in their language(s), about their religion(s), culture(s), and technologies.

Conclusion

My library experiences have led me to discover an inspiring corollary to Ranganthan's (2006) five laws:

1. Books are for use.

2. Every reader his or her book.

3. Every book its reader.

4. Save the time of the reader.

5. A library is a growing organism.

6. Corollary: A growing library experiences growing pains and becomes transformational.

Supporting global south publishing with de-northernization, undertaking individual unconscious bias training, and institutional prioritization of DEI are not easy or comfortable. Using the principle of "think globally, act locally" to incorporate DEI and equity-minded preparatory practices will transform our libraries and institutions. These practices will nurture a keen appreciation of the global landscape of users, cultures, and collection items in collection development librarians. Such librarians will change unjust systems of epistemic supremacy in librarianship and help build just libraries for all people.

Works Cited

Abioye, Abiola, and Sunday Abiodun Oluwaniyi. 2017. "Collection Development and Preservation Of Indigenous Knowledge in Selected Federal University Libraries in South West, Nigeria." *Library Philosophy and Practice* 163. *https://digitalcommons.unl. edu/libphilprac/163.*

American Library Association. n.d. "Equity, Diversity, Inclusion: An Interpretation of the Library Bill of Rights." *https://ala.org/advocacy/intfreedom/librarybill/interpretations/EDI.*

Anti-racism Digital Library. 2022. *https://sacred.omeka.net.*

Australian Institute of Aboriginal and Torres Strait Islanders. 2021. *Pathways: Gateway to the AIATSIS Thesauri. https://www1.aiatsis. gov.au.*

Art & Architecture Thesaurus Online. 2022. *https://getty.edu/research/tools/vocabularies/aat.*

Atla Digital Library. 2022. *https://dl.atla.com.*

Carmack, Nan. 2021. "Collecting for Diversity, Equity, Inclusion: Best Practices for Virginia Libraries." *Virginia Libraries* 65, no. 1: 5. *https://doi.org/10.21061/valib.v65i1.622.*

Center for the Study of Global Christianity. 2022. *https://gordonconwell.edu.*

Cooke, Nicole. 2020. "What It Means to Decolonize the Library." *Publishers Weekly. https://publishersweekly.com/pw/by-topic/industry-news/libraries/article/85127-what-it-means-to-decolonize-the-library.html.*

Darby, Kristy. 2019. "Acquiring Open Access Children's Books." *The Signal. https://blogs.loc.gov/thesignal/2019/07/acquiring-open-access-childrens-books.*

Dyas-Correaia, S., and Reas Devakos. 2014. "Open Access and Collection Development Policies: Two Solitudes." *https://library.ifla.org/id/eprint/839/1/108-correia-en.pdf.*

Engelson, Leslie. 2015. "Collection Development." *https://youtu.be/Kx8k2e6qyh8.*

IFLA/UNESCO. 2012. "Multicultural Library Manifesto: The Multicultural Library – A Gateway to a Culturally Diverse Society in Dialogue." *https://repository.ifla.org/handle/123456789/731.*

International Federation of Library Associations and Institutions. 2021. "Get into the 2005 Convention on the Protection and Promotion of the Diversity of Cultural Expressions." *https://repository.ifla.org/handle/123456789/308.*

Internet Archive. 2022. Spirituality and Religion Collection, Moving Image Archive. *https://archive.org/details/spiritualityandreligion.*

Johnson, Sharon et al. 2012. "Key Issues for E-Resource Collection Development: A Guide for Libraries." *https://repository.ifla.org/handle/123456789/194.*

Labeodan, Helen. 2016. "Revisiting the Legacy of the Circle of Concerned African Women Theologians Today: A Lesson in Strength and Perseverance." *Verbum et Ecclesia. https://scielo.org.za/pdf/vee/v37n2/08.pdf.*

Living Tongues Institute for Endangered Languages. 2022. *https://livingtongues.org.*

Mbambo-Thata, Buhle, Jia Tina Du, Ulrike Lang, Jesús Lau, Amal W. Mostafa, Bharat Mehra, Clara M. Chu, and Jaya Raju. 2019. "Gender Inclusivity and Equity in Academic Libraries: Insights from Around the Globe." *College and Research Libraries News Online,* September.

Miller, Mary E., and Suzanne M. Ward. 2022. "Rightsizing Your Collection." *American Libraries,* May: 40–4.

OAPEN: Open Access Publishing in European Networks. 2022. *https://library.oapen.org.*

Patheos Library of World Religions and Faith Traditions. 2022. *https://patheos.com/library.*

Ranganathan, S.R. 2006. *The Five Laws of Library Science.* Reprint. Bangalore: Sarada Ranganathan Endowment in Library Science.

Remy, Charlie. 2018. "Autistics in the Library: How Libraries Can More Effectively Serve Patrons and Employees on the Spectrum." *https://vimeo.com/289356971.*

Smith, Audrey C., Leandra Merz, Jesse B. Borden, Chris Gulick, Akhil R. Kshirsagar, and Emilio M. Bruna. 2020. "Assessing the Effect of Article Processing Charges on the Geographic Diversity of Authors Using Elsevier's 'Mirror Journal' System." MetaArXiv, September 2. *https://doi.org/10.31222/osf.io/s7cx4.*

UNESCO. 2005. Convention of the Protection and Promotion of the Diversity of Cultural Expressions.

WNDB. 2014. "We Need Diverse Books." *https://diversebooks.org/about-wndb.*

Zecker, Robert M. 2013. *Racism and America's Immigrant Press: How the Slovaks Were Taught to Think Like White People.* Bloomsbury.

Emerging Practices

CHAPTER 6

Beginning the Theological Library

ELIZABETH A. LEAHY

*T*HEOLOGICAL LIBRARIES, AS WELL AS THEOLOGICAL COLLECTIONS WITHIN AN EX-isting library, all start somewhere. A library might begin with a small collection of books given by a professor or an alumnus, or possibly with a recognized need within your organization to begin a collection.

Perhaps this is the challenge before you—how to begin to put together the resources that will be useful for the learning context you are in and develop the type of collections that will inform and shape the religious/theological studies taught at your institution. On the other hand, perhaps you are beginning in a position in an established library and are entrusted with continuing the work and growing the collections further. Whichever circumstance you may find yourself in, my hope is that this chapter will provide ideas and practical help.

Context and Calling

As institutions differ, so do their libraries. Spending the time to learn and understand the culture of your institution is critical. If you are working in a library within your religious/theological tradition, you may have some background already—but taking the time to get to know long-time faculty and reading resources on the tradition can be invaluable as you consider how to shape the collection. This orientation becomes even more important if your background differs from that of your institution.

Theological schools have a variety of reasons for existing—to train clergy and laity for the practical skills of ministry, to develop academicians and scholars, to train educators and missionaries, and to provide programs for spiritual nurture and development. Your institution may do one or more of these activities, each of which may require unique resources.

Your school may be a small stand-alone Bible institute or a larger religious/theological school, possibly situated within another academic institution. Some librarians may have strong theological backgrounds through advanced studies and others may be entering into an area of great interest but with a limited background. The first theological library that I worked in and developed was in a ministry organization with a small number of books that required some organization. We had few resources at hand—and I had neither a theological degree nor one in librarianship—so I had much to learn!

Academic culture at each institution may also differ. Accordingly, the role of the librarian may vary considerably from one type of institution to another. Expectations for who has oversight for collection development may be different as well. If we look at a range of institutions, it is rare that librarian roles and collections are conceived of in exactly the same way.

Collection Assessment

When looking for a place to begin, a good first step is to assess the collection. Is it a well-defined collection built up over years—or, more often, a bit of a hodge-podge with some areas of strength and much-needed opportunities for growth?

Collection assessment has a number of components—the first consideration is determining whom your collection serves (your context). Is the focus primarily on the students and secondarily on the faculty (or the reverse)? Do you have additional community users such as local religious leaders? Do you have partnerships with other institutions in your faith tradition or in your geographic area?

Library director Jim Agee (2005) writes that "collection evaluations help librarians better realize what materials are in their collections, and how well they are meeting their collection development goals" and sees collection evaluation as one important measure of collection development. He adds: "A properly implemented evaluation may help focus concerns, uncover the character of the collection already in place, reveal gaps, measure the currency and historical depth of the collection, or reflect accuracy of vendor profiles—used for slip or approval plans—in meeting collection goals."

Talk to your users. Recognize that this may mean that you need to spend time outside of the library to learn more of what is needed. Get input from classroom faculty about what is working or what is missing. Review their syllabi to see the recommended and required resources, and consider items that will supplement each course. What are the research or teaching interests of your faculty and administration? How current is the collection, and when has it been weeded?

Collection assessment is an ongoing concern for librarians—it is never "a one and done" activity. As collection development depends heavily upon the budget that a library has, most libraries have some form of assessment underway on an ongoing basis. This might include an overall review and then looking at specific areas of the collection for in-depth review each year. If the library has a primary focus in curricular support, certain course syllabi and discipline areas can be selected each year—books of scripture, history of the faith tradition, preaching and teaching, etc. Over a several-year period, the entire collection can undergo a review.

Curricular Support

For library collections that are designed to support the curriculum, you should look first at the resources that the students are expected to have accessible. Depending upon the situation of your school and your students, students may not be able to afford individual purchases of texts. If the latter, the library should attempt to own one or more copies of the needed titles. Print copies might be placed on reserve, or, if the school has the capacity for e-books, these might be considered for purchase as well. If the students and the library have reliable internet access, the librarian can work closely with faculty members to encourage adoption of texts that are open access, bringing down the cost for students and for the library budget.

As you review the syllabi, consider the listed assignments—will there be research papers or presentations? Shorter reports such as book reviews? Would it be helpful to have examples from various traditions? For instance, if a course is on preaching, the collection would be enhanced not only with the required texts but also with resources that show different styles/methods, possibly sample sermons and/or sermon illustrations. A course on the history of the church in a particular geographic area can be enhanced with biographies of church leaders or missionaries, histories of the religious organizations in the area, creedal and denominational histories, and critical works that analyze the period studied.

In many instances, this kind of expansive look may only lead the librarian to a few new selections in each area due to budget constraints. The work involved is still important as it can assist in setting priorities for purchases or gift selections in the future. Theological libraries are typically not built overnight—but an awareness of curricular needs can be of great assistance as you plan for both short and long-term growth.

Role of a Collection Development Policy

Whether you are beginning the library or continuing the work, having a functional collection development policy can be a key resource for funding and gift decisions. Policies can vary greatly in length and scope—some policies are a page or two and state how the library will support the mission of the school through the collections. Other policies can be extensive and might list the key subject disciplines and the level to which these materials are collected. In a small library, a short policy could highlight the disciplinary areas you plan to collect (and perhaps, what you do not); the types of materials, such as print books, electronic books, journals, databases, and media types; and how you plan to handle gifts of resources to the library. Because media types can change rapidly, it is wise to update your plan as media changes (for instance, moving from VHS tapes to DVDs). If your library has space constraints, having a plan for weeding the collection to maintain currency is also good to include.

A thoughtful collection development policy can take some work at the outset, but it is invaluable for goal setting over time. If a donor wants to give your library a collection that doesn't fit your mission or space, you will have a written document that shows you have given consideration to what will be best for the school overall and be able to kindly refuse the gift. If your administration is raising funds for academics, having plans for what will improve your collection may be helpful. Finally, these policies are often requested if your school is being reviewed for an accreditation and can help accreditors direct administrators' attention to library needs. There are excellent resources on preparing different types of collection development policies and many schools have their policy on a library website—so you can get a sense of what might work best in your institution.

Joys and Challenges of Donated and Gift Materials

Many schools rely upon donated print books and journals to grow their collection. Depending upon the original collector of the materials, this may be a boon for your library—or may be a time-consuming project to find the small number of materials that can be valuable. Gifts follow the interests of the giver, so having some knowledge of the giver is helpful in determining if the gift might be a match. If it is feasible, ask if you might see the items before they are packed up and delivered to your front door. Clarify within your organization that you are the one to make the decision on whether the gift is to be accepted (and having the collection development policy in place is a help here). This is not always possible, of course. Sometimes a donor will give their library linked with a donation to the school. If you think this might be possible, it is wise to work with the office that handles your financial donations.

There is not a single policy on the best ways to handle gift collections. Gift books can arrive in excellent condition or can be covered in dust and have mold issues. The librarian will need to review each title, decide if it is acceptable for the collection, catalog and process it. Gifts are time-consuming projects. Much depends upon the budget you have and the amount of time you can allocate to processing collections. No gift is "free"—even if the books are.

Collaboration with Administration

When we think of collection development, the first thing that springs to mind is not usually the role of administrators. And yet, they can play key roles in how collections are both developed and utilized. Much depends on the context and size of your institution.

Clearly, a librarian who works singly in a stand-alone theological school will have a significantly different experience than one who works as part of a team within a larger university setting. Yet both librarians will find their work enhanced through collaboration with colleagues.

Dr. Debbie Creamer writes on the importance of librarians learning how to be a translator or interpreter to their colleagues. Most academics train in the scholarship of their discipline and perhaps, to a lesser degree, in teaching. Very few have training or background in administrative skills—something that librarians often take for granted. We learn principles of organizing resources, working with budgets, and—in larger libraries—supervising others. We work with or write plans and policies and may be involved with accreditation. However, our academic colleagues will not know about these skills if we are quiet. Creamer suggests reporting in meetings about the administrative work you are doing, in addition to reports on the collections. If there is an opportunity to do so, serve on committees within your institution. These committees can serve as bridge-builders to allow others to get to know more about you and the library and allow you to advocate for what your library needs to be successful (Keck, Bidlack, and Creamer, 2019). The one caution is that your committee work must not continually take precedence over your work in developing the library.

Connections in administration can be very helpful as the institutional budget is planned or as funds are raised and grants are written. Think of this effort as developing advocates for your library. The more an administrator can speak knowledgeably about the library, the better. When others in your institution are aware of the work that you (and your colleagues) are accomplishing in the library and are aware of the resources needed, you stand a better chance of receiving what is needed.

If your school has an individual whose work involves writing grants, take the time to get to know them and introduce them to your library. Sometimes a library purchase can be added to a grant in process. For instance, if a faculty member is writing a grant for a project, adding some funding for resources to support that project may be quite feasible. Perhaps a donor to your institution suggests an undesignated gift in memory of someone special. If administrators working with grants and donors are aware that you have a wish list, you might be pleasantly surprised to receive funding for some items. The key is to be prepared.

Collaboration with Teaching Faculty

Exactly what does collaboration look like in the academic environment? Pham and Tanner (2014, 23) have defined collaboration between librarians and academic colleagues as "an educationally innovative process among academics, librarians and other relevant parties who are working together to share knowledge and expertise to support the enhancement of teaching, learning and research experiences for the university community."

Context is important here as well. The role of the librarian in selection of materials for the library may be affected by differences between schools, cultural differences between countries, and even between departments. In their work reflecting upon three libraries in Hong Kong, Ferguson, Nesta, and Storey write:

> The role of the librarian, for example, in collection development might vary considerably. While in large libraries in North America, collection development librarians might be responsible for selecting 90+ percent of what is bought, in a place like Hong Kong they might have to get a faculty member to approve every book. (Ferguson, Nesta and Storey 2007, 222)

It is important to realize that many, if not most, of your academic colleagues may have a limited understanding of what your library offers or how it is organized. This limitation may be predicated upon their experience at another institution. As new faculty are hired, make the effort to get to know them. I see this annually as a new opportunity to share about our library collections and programs—to distinguish our library from ones they might have been affiliated with in the past. Think about ways to connect your collection and programs with their teaching and research interests.

While much of the literature on collaboration with faculty involves bibliographic instruction, there is still an important role in working with faculty to develop their advocacy for a strong library collection. Consider opportunities to bring faculty into the library for meetings, have small celebrations, and highlight new additions to your collection. Get to know the research and teaching interests of your colleagues by scheduling time with them over coffee or tea, and through this find ways to connect the library to what they are doing. The more that these colleagues know about the collections and what the library is attempting to do, the more helpful they can be in encouraging students to use the resources and making recommendations for good additions. Faculty members may also be aware of their colleagues at other institutions who may be retiring and seeking to contribute their personal library collections somewhere. Perhaps those collections might find a home in your library.

Collaboration with Library Networks and Associations

One of the finest traits of librarians is the generosity they have in sharing ideas and resources with others, not only with those in their own institutions but with other librarians in the same geographic area, and even through international collaboration. I have personally benefited through my involvement with Atla and locally with the Southern California Theological Library Association (SCATLA). Each organization has enabled me to gain from the expertise of others while giving me opportunities to share my resources and expertise, too. When I was a new theological librarian beginning a library, several library directors in the area reached out to me and offered duplicate journals from their collection to assist my small start-up collection.

In a study of library directors and key librarians in Oman, participants expressed interest in collaborative relationships at both the institutional and individual level. The writers found "The three most important advantages of collaboration were emphasized. They are: to enlarge and improve the library services, including increasing users' access to interlibrary information resources; to reduce costs by sharing manpower and resources; and to share experience through communication and enhance skills and knowledge of staff through collaborative training" (Al-Harrasi and Al-Aufi 2012, 240). Depending on both the location and collection type, librarians can also investigate collaborative collection development, where two or more libraries commit to purchasing certain unique titles that can be made available to all of the libraries in the collecting group.

However, not all parts of the world have ready access to regional networks of librarians. Julia Gross and Aminath Riyaz (2004) detail a collaboration between an academic library in Western Australia and one in the Republic of Maldives, brought together through a Link Institution project funded by the World Bank. Their project seeks to increase library resources and training in countries with limited numbers of trained librarians, improve access to collections, and help to set standards in place with collection development goals. If a library has at least some internet access, finding librarians who are willing to assist with questions no longer requires geographic proximity. For theological librarians, there are a variety of networks internationally, including Atla, ANZTLA (Australia and New Zealand), BETH (Europe), and ForATL (Forum of Asian Theological Librarianship). There are also other associations of academic and/or specialized librarians (outside of the religious/theological studies arena), so it is advantageous to see if your library might participate. Not only will you form new friendships, but you will find opportunities to learn from one another and to strengthen collections that can advance the work of your school.

Works Cited

Agee, Jim. 2005. "Collection Evaluation: A Foundation for Collection Development." *Collection Building* 24, no. 3: 92–5. *https://doi.org/10.1108/01604950510608267.*

Al-Harrasi, Nabhan, and Ali AlAufi. 2012. "The Potential of InterState Collaboration for Omani Academic Libraries." *Library Review* 61, no. 4: 240-60. *https://doi.org/10.1108/00242531211267554.*

Dempsey, Lorcan, Constance Malpus, and Brian Lavoie. 2014. "Collection Directions: the Evolution of Library Collections and Collecting." *Portal: Libraries and the Academy* 14, no. 3: 393–423. *https://doi.org/10.1353/pla.2014.0013*.

Duncan, Cheri Jeanette, and Genya Morgan O'Gara. 2015. "Building Holistic and Agile Collection Development and Assessment." *Performance Measurement and Metrics* 16, no. 1: 62–79. *https://doi.org/10.1108/PMM-12-2014-0041*.

Ferguson, Anthony, Frederick Nesta, and Colin Storey. 2007. "Managing Across Cultures: The Experiences of Three Hong Kong Academic Library Directors." *Library Management* 25, no. 4/5: 213–33. *https://doi.org/10.1108/01435120710744164*.

Gross, Julia, and Aminath Riyaz. 2004. "An Academic Library Partnership in the Indian Ocean Region." *Library Review* 53, no. 4: 220–27. *https://doi.org/10.1108/00242530410531848*.

Horava, Tony, and Michael Levine-Clark. 2016. "Current Trends in Collection Development Practices and Policies." *Collection Building* 35, no. 4: 97–102. *https://doi.org/10.1108/CB-09-2016-0025*.

Keck, Andrew, Beth Bidlack, and Debbie Creamer. 2019. "The View from the Dean's Office." *Atla Summary of Proceedings* 73: 102–14. *https://doi.org/10.31046/proceedings.2019.1612*.

Kusik, James P., and Mark A. Vargas. 2009. "Implementing a 'Holistic' Approach to Collection Development." *Library Leadership & Management* 23, no. 4: 186–92. *https://doi.org/10.5860/llm.v23i4.1794*

McMahon, Melody Layton. 2004. "Librarians and Teaching Faculty in Collaboration: New Incentives, New Opportunities." *Theological Education* 40, no. 1: 73–87. *https://ats.edu/files/galleries/2004-theological-education-v40-n1.pdf*.

Pham, Hue Thi, and Kerry Tanner. 2014. "Collaboration between Academics and Librarians: A Literature Review and Framework for Analysis." *Library Review* 63, no. 1/2: 15–45. *https://doi.org/10.1108/LR-06-2013-0064*.

CHAPTER 7

Collection Assessment Is for Everyone!

TAMMY JOHNSON

WHO NEEDS COLLECTION ASSESSMENT? EVERYONE! CUSTOMARILY, LIBRARIES acquire new materials through both purchases and gifts. A tenet commonly held in libraries is that none of these materials should ever be thrown away. However, collection development is an active term; it implies the collection is constantly being reshaped through acquisitions and weeding, growing in some areas and shrinking in others. One method of determining if the collection is timely and useful for the library's current constituencies is to do an assessment of the collection. Collection assessment is the tool that provides the data or information to shape the collection. Collection assessment asks questions such as, "Should all the items that are currently in our library be part of the collection?" or, "Does that pastoral care book from 1953 really contain information that contributes to the knowledge of 21st-century practitioners?" For a vibrant, growing collection, assessment should always accompany collection development.

Why Collection Assessment?

Collections are made to be used. This does not mean, however, that collections gathered over the years have the materials that support their communities' actual use today or support the curriculum and mission of their institutions. Since usage and users change over time, the collections must evolve to match those changes. Collection assessment makes this evolution possible. Information gleaned from assessments can contribute to overall collection development goals. For example, if a previous collection development policy states that there is a strength in a subject area, an assessment of that subject area can determine if the strength still exists.

The term *assessment* can be daunting. Sometimes it is immediately equated with huge costs and considerable amounts of personnel time. Yet, there are many types of assessment that can be done with the local catalog or software on hand in most libraries. The assessments can be structured in a manner that does not demand many staff hours, so that resources can be deployed for an assessment in a manner that aligns with a given library's financial realities. Intentionally designed assessments can, therefore, maximize the resources already at a library's disposal to account for most of the necessary elements of assessment.

Information or data is an integral part of the assessment. Data about the collection allows for an analysis that answers an assessment's questions and helps library staff achieve assessment goals. Data can be gathered using either quantitative or qualitative techniques, or both.

Quantitative measures involve numerical inquiries about a library. These methods may include usage statistics for access, comparisons of titles, and budget numbers (Kohn 2015, 13–14). Circulation numbers can also provide useful information about usage of library materials, while an investigation of interlibrary loan statistics may give clues to gaps within a collection. Other quantitative data is also accessible within the library's environment. Network information from logons can reveal whether acquired materials are being accessed. Authentication tools such as Open Athens and OCLC's EZ

Proxy Analytics provide usage and user information. Counting Online Usage of Networked Electronic Resources (COUNTER), a system generally used by vendors such as JSTOR, Brill, and Alexander Street Press, also supplies user access data to customers. The software indicates which titles are accessed, which are turned away, and any access denials. Cost-per-use statistics can be derived from COUNTER reports (Mellins-Cohen n.d., 3). Data on access and cost is valuable for collection development decisions by providing information for decision making regarding future purchases, subscriptions, and weeding the collection.

The quality of a collection can also be another area of assessment. Qualitative data methods include using devices such as surveys, focus groups, library narratives, or other means of investigation that give insight into the way patrons value the collection (Kohn 2015, 6–7). Administering user surveys is a means to amass data about library collections. For example, a survey may ask questions such as "Is the collection robust enough to support user needs for a given topic?" or "Are print titles preferable to e-books?" Even asking patrons questions like "Do you use library serials?" will reveal information about the library collection's usage. Sometimes it is best to use a combination of qualitative and quantitative information. Kelly and O'Gara (2018, 20) suggest using such a combination or a "holistic approach." This type of assessment examines the formats of a collection and its use by the library. A "holistic approach" provides a larger view than a single subject or a subset of users; it examines the entirety of all involved in the endeavor, both users and materials. Clarifying what type of measurement to use—quantitative or qualitative or both—helps lay the foundation for a successful assessment. Since any given library is inundated with internal and external data, the key is selecting the proper data that supports the assessment being performed.

Elements of Collection Assessment

A successful assessment organizes the methods and data in a manner or narrative that can lead to useful information about the collection. The process begins by asking a question about the collection. The next step is to use that question to formulate a goal that is tied to the mission of the library. The goal can be used to decide if the measurement should be qualitative, quantitative, or a combination of the two. This step is followed by creating or using an assessment tool or process that will complete the goal and answer the question. Next, the information is gathered and the assessment is done. Then findings should be shared with pertinent persons. The final step is to take actions indicated by the assessment findings.

Developing the Question or Subject of the Assessment

As mentioned above, the process begins by asking a question about the collection to determine what needs to be answered (Kohn 2015, 2–3). A question that is too broad can lead to inaction or mismanagement of resources due to the scope of the activity. The question should be derived from the library's context. A database that has heavy usage in one library may not have the same usage in another library. For example, say it is time to renew a subscription for database X. Library A may automatically renew because every month the statistics reveal very heavy usage. Library B will have to do an assessment because the usage data is not as readily available. Therefore, the question for library B might be, "Are online users using database X?" A focused assessment can lead to a specific answer that can lead to an action to improve the collection, either by weeding, by adding titles, or by making other adjustments (3–4).

Creating the Assessment Goal

After formulating the question, the assessor creates a goal. The goal could also be as simple as, "Determine if library B should renew database X." On the other hand, any given library may have a more complex goal, such as "The goal is to determine whether database X can be dropped and if the subsequent funds saved can be used to buy other necessary resources." A clearly defined goal helps organize the project around the proper assessment method for investigation. Thus, such a goal will "guide the process" (Gregory 2019, 106).

Selecting the Assessment Tool

After the goal is determined, the assessment tool must be selected. If a tool is not readily available through previous assessments or subscriptions, the assessor determines tools, software, processes, or devices that can be used to do the assessment and fit within the realm of the resources available to the library. Since libraries are set in a specific context, each assessment requires tailoring the study to specific conditions and goals. Elmer E. Rasmuson Library at the University of Alaska Fairbanks offers an example of using a qualitative assessment method. The library had hired a full-time person to repair circulating books. However, the number of books sent for repair was lower than anticipated (Rinio 2016, 193). The librarians suspected that a large number of items needing repairs were being reshelved rather than routed to the repair person, so they created a two-part assessment of the collection to determine if there was a need to employ a full-time repair person. One part of the assessment examined the physical condition of the entire collection and another part examined the condition of circulating books. The assessment revealed that indeed many of the circulating books should not have been re-shelved upon return to the library. Several items were damaged and should have been routed to the technician (207). A qualitative assessment tool selected in the case at Rasmuson was the proper tool to use in that context.

Reporting the Assessment Findings

Once the assessment is completed, the results are shared with others. Depending on the reporting structure within the organization, information can be shared with your team, supervisor, or other parties in the library. The assessment data may indicate that budgetary resources are needed to address the issues found in the collection. Personnel training may be needed. Even if a librarian is in a one-person shop, there may be other stakeholders such as administrators, faculty, or students that could benefit from learning about the outcomes of an assessment.

Post-assessment Actions

The last thing to do is take necessary actions indicated by the assessment and the existing collection development policies. For example, if an assessment reported that database X had little use, the action may indicate the database should be dropped. The library may need to replace database X with a different database to fulfill the collection development needs in a given subject area.

Not every assessment has to be designed and carried out by a sole library. Vendors or various library associations may also be able to provide statistics, software, or other tools to be used in examining a library's holdings. For example, Gold Rush, a product of the Colorado Alliance of Research Libraries, has software that can be used in assessments. The product contains title lists from several sources. This component allows the titles of a library to be compared against other title lists from services including aggregators, publishers, and indexing and abstracting sources (Colorado n.d.). The fee for Gold Rush's MARC record comparison tool can range from free to "at cost" (Machovec 2021). Eastern Academic Scholars' Trust (EAST), an organization concerned with maintaining a collaborative print collection for long-term access, used Gold Rush to analyze the number of member library holdings to identify any unique titles and any overlap (Stearns 2021).

Some vendor products may have costs associated with usage. Worldshare Collection Evaluation, available through the OCLC Worldshare Platform, may be used for collection analysis. The program allows participating libraries to examine their own holdings and compare holdings with other libraries. An institution can use title lists to identify unique and shared titles. The library's subscription level with OCLC determines its cost of access to the Worldshare Collection Evaluation product (OCLC n.d.).

Proquest also has an assessment tool called the Intota Assessment Platform. The product is distributed by ExLibris Knowledge Center, a Proquest company. The Intota Assessment Platform provides quick access to usage statistics such as COUNTER reports for e-books and journals with turn-away data, usage by fund, and database information. Library reports include cost by subject, publisher, and circulation data. Intota also has a component named 360 Usage Statistics that provides title-by-title information for journals and databases.

The various features of the Intota Assessment Platform are available depending upon the subscription level of the library (Proquest, n.d.).

Lack of funding or the inability to acquire external vendor resources should not be a deterrent to collection assessment, however. Free tools and workflows can be adapted to answer some of the questions of assessment. Many characteristics of a collection can be revealed by simply using the local catalog or integrated library system (ILS). Reports can be run for certain classification areas or subject headings for lists of titles in that area. A combination of reports with circulation counts and classification and/or subject headings can reveal which materials from an area in the library have circulated. Acquisition reports can be created to determine areas of large costs. If the goal is to reduce expenditures in a library, the ILS can provide a comparison of costs within the various fund codes. A great deal of useful assessment data about the collection, then, can be derived from the ILS.

Librarians are the most valuable sources of information about assessments, assessment tools, or processes. Formal or informal assessments are generally ongoing in many libraries. Questions about expenditures, weeding, space for new materials, formats, and so forth are central to the continuous process of collection development. Thus, consulting with and learning from librarians at other institutions, regional associations, or consortia can be a fruitful way of refining and enriching your own assessment process.

Example of an Assessment

The collections staff at John Bulow Campbell Library (JBCL) at Columbia Theological Seminary (CTS) used an assessment strategy that has been employed at libraries worldwide—a comparison between the local catalog and catalogs at other institutions. Quick questions regarding collection development funds needed to be answered. A free assessment would save time and money. Recently, CTS added an online component to its Master of Arts (Theological Studies) (MATS) degree program. A MATS student can now seek a degree as an online-only student or as a residential student. The program has five areas of concentration: Old Testament, New Testament, theology, church history, and ethics (MA(TS), n.d.). To support the addition of an online component to the MATS degree program, the library was given a slight budget increase. Allocation of these new funds needed to happen judiciously. The question was whether additional online reference materials might need to be purchased for each area. An assessment of each program area was needed to determine if the existing online reference titles in the CTS library catalog were adequate for the new program.

In order to keep the assessment manageable in terms of time and personnel, the church history area was chosen as the first area of assessment. Over the years, this program had been well supported by acquisitions, making it the best area to examine first. Therefore, the goal of the assessment was to determine whether CTS has adequate online reference materials to support the church history online MATS program. Lessons learned from this assessment could be used for examining the other areas of the MATS. The assessment goal ties into CTS's mission to prepare students for leadership in ministry in the world (CTS n.d., "Mission"). The titles would be limited to Christianity, as most of the students at CTS are Christian. Furthermore, only titles from the last five years would be included in the assessment to increase the probability that the titles would still be available for purchase if necessary. The assessment was done by comparing titles in the CTS catalog with titles in peer libraries. A qualitative assessment used existing and available resources. A single staff person, the librarian that works in collection development, did the assessment. No cost was associated with checking catalogs. Peer comparison of similar libraries using lists was the best fit for this assessment because it offered verifiable evidence of the presence of reference titles purchased by other libraries.

The library catalogs of five seminary or divinity libraries were examined. The Association for Theological Schools (ATS) website and information gathered from the CTS administrative body helped determine which five libraries would serve as peer libraries. Two of the five were considered peer institutions due to similar areas of study, similar historical denominational ties, and similar seminary community sizes. The other three were larger and considered by some to be the "standard bearers," or some of the best theological libraries in the country. The larger schools' libraries are considered aspirational peers and served as controls for the evaluation. If a title found in a peer library was not found in either of the larger libraries, further study would be warranted. For example, the publisher and publication year, as well as how the title might fit into the MATS program, were areas considered.

After the peers were selected, the assessment was ready to start. Titles were searched in the similarly sized libraries' catalogs and then searched in the larger libraries' catalogs. One Library of Congress subject heading, Church History, served as the search term. The term was combined with two subdivisions: Encyclopedias and Dictionaries. The terms were used as subject headings and also searched as title and keyword combinations: "church history encyclopedia" and "church history dictionary." The last search examined the subject heading and each subdivision term singularly as a keyword and title search. Each search was limited to the specific area of the history of Christian churches. Limiters were used if available in the catalog to fit the specifications of the assessment. For example, if the term "dictionary" was searched, the limiters used were "Christianity," "electronic," or "e-books" and "date range including the years 2017 to 2021." After a list of titles was compiled from the findings, the titles were then searched in the CTS catalog.

The comparisons of lists of reference titles in Christian church history proved to be useful by identifying titles that did and did not need to be added to the CTS online collection. For instance, each of the peer institutions and two of the three larger institutions owned an encyclopedia on early Christianity that CTS did not own in print. However, CTS had access to an e-book version of the title through a subscription, so no action needed to be taken for the collection with regard to that title at this time. Another encyclopedia on the history of Christianity in the United States was held by each of the five libraries. One of the peer institutions and one of the larger libraries had e-book holdings of the title. CTS owned a print copy of the encyclopedia. After gathering more information on the book owned by all the libraries, the assessor determined that CTS should buy the online reference edition for the online MATS church history concentration. The assessment, in this case, led to an action that addressed a collection development need. The result was shared with acquisitions so that the necessary title could be purchased.

Conclusion

Everyone needs collection assessment. Students change, curricula change, and the culture changes, so the collection must change. Though there may be a case in a specific context when a library needs to pay for a tool in order to perform an assessment, neither the assessment at Rasmusson nor the assessment at CTS had exorbitant financial strings attached. Regardless of the cost, it is important to remember that the library holdings have to be tended to. As the collection grows, it must be weeded. Assessment tools, whether paid or free, can lead to a vibrant, thriving collection. Colleagues, vendors, and the local ILS may provide the tools for assessment. Whether it be a large, complex look at the collection or a small examination of a degree area, an assessment can help keep the collection dynamic and evolving as it seeks to continually serve its community.

Works Cited

Colorado Alliance of Research Libraries. n.d. "Gold Rush Decision Support." Accessed October 31, 2021. *https://coalliance.org/gold-rush-product-descriptions.*

Columbia Theological Seminary. n.d. "Master of Arts (Theological Studies)-MA(TS)." *https://ctsnet.edu/degree-program/master-of-arts-theological-studies-mats.*

———. n.d. "Statement of Mission." Accessed November 27, 2021. *https://ctsnet.edu/about-us/columbia-academics.*

Gregory, Vicki L. 2019. *Collection Development and Management for 21st Century Library Collections: An Introduction.* Second Edition. Chicago: ALA Neal-Schuman.

Kelly, Madeline, and Genya O'Gara. 2018. "Collections Assessment: Developing Sustainable Programs and Projects." *Serials Librarian* 74, nos. 1–4: 19–29. *https://doi.org/10.1080/036152 6X.2018.1428453.*

Kohn, Karen C. 2015. *Collection Evaluation in Academic Libraries: A Practical Guide for Librarians.* Lanham: Rowman & Littlefield.

Machovec, George. "Gold Rush Analytics" at Analyzing Collections Using Gold Rush Webinar. Accessed on YouTube video embedded link 1:17:02; viewed on October 31, 2021. *https://sharedprint. org/2021/10/06/analyzing-collections-using-gold-rush.*

Mellins-Cohen, Tasha. "Release 5.0.2: The Friendly Guide for Librarians." COUNTER. Accessed on November 24, 2021. *https://project-counter.org/wp-content/uploads/2021/09/Release5.0.2_FG_Librarians_v4.pdf.*

OCLC. n.d. "Worldshare Collection Evaluation." Accessed October 31, 2021. *https://help.oclc.org/Library_Management/WorldShare_Collection_Evaluation.*

Proquest. n.d. ExLibris Knowledge Center, 360 Services, "Intota Assessment: Introduction and Overview of the Intota Assessment Platform." Accessed November 6, 2021. *https://knowledge.exlibris-group.com/360_Services/360_Core_Client_Center/0Product_Documentation/Reports/360_Services%2C_Intota_Assessment%3A_Introduction_and_Overview_of_the_Intota_Assessment_Platform.*

Rinio, Tyson. 2016. "Collection Condition Assessment in a Midsized Academic Library." *Collection Management* 41, no. 4: 193–208. *https://doi.org/10.1080/01462679.2016.1227289.*

Stearns, Susan, and Sara Amato. 2021. "Analyzing Collections for Shared Print" at Analyzing Collections Using Gold Rush Webinar, October 31. Accessed on YouTube video embedded link 1:17:02; viewed on October 31, 2021. *https://sharedprint.org/2021/10/06/analyzing-collections-using-gold-rush.*

CHAPTER 8

Reference Sources for Small Seminaries

Prospects and Challenges

YESAN SELLAN

A CQUIRING REFERENCE SOURCES IS OFTEN A CHALLENGING TASK FOR SMALL LI-braries due to lack of established procedures involved in acquisition. This essay attempts to answer questions related to the development of reference sources in small seminary libraries. Small libraries can be defined as theological libraries that have five or fewer full time equivalent staff and/or serve institutions with an enrollment of less than 200 FTE (Stephens 2016, 29). The scholarly productivity of academia depends on the availability of balanced reference sources accessible through their libraries.

How can I improve my library's reference collections? How might I acquire more reference resources for the library with a minimum investment? Will the current library resources suffice to support the programmes my institution offers, now and in the future? These are some of the daunting questions the librarians and administrators of small theological institutions are likely to ask.

The library supports the academic pursuits of the faculty members and students by providing a carefully curated collection of resources. Absence of quality learning resources would make a library simply a storeroom with books. Academic libraries exist to achieve the mission and vision of the institutions they serve. Libraries have a mandate to contribute to the growth and development of teaching and learning activities of the faculty members, students, and alumni/ae. Stephens (2016, 31) aptly reiterates that seminary libraries exist to cater to the information needs of their patrons, particularly the groups mentioned above, by understanding who they are and what they need. Therefore, when acquiring learning resources, an academic library must carefully endeavor to fill any gaps in the reference collection and avoid adding irrelevant, redundant resources. The collective and collaborative efforts of the faculty members, administrators, and the librarians can help identify relevant sources and thus help improve reference services offered by libraries.

Developing library resources in general requires systematic planning and the execution of clear policies. The collection development policy of a library plays a major role in developing its holdings. It is the responsibility of the librarians to develop and adopt a collection development policy, in consultation with the faculty members, for their libraries. The collection development policy of a library reflects the institution's mission and vision. Thus, the library collection development policy plays a major role in providing practical guidelines for the library staff, enabling them to add learning resources systematically and weed out resources that do not meet the needs of the users. The acquisition of a good reference collection is an important task of the librarians to address the information needs of library patrons. Librarians' knowledge of current trends in the theological disciplines and familiarity with the acquisition process help them strengthen their library's resources. As Hattendorf (1989, 228) rightly notes, the development of a reference collection is an art when it is done well.

The Importance of the Reference Collection

in a Seminary Library

As Kansfield (1980, 83) observes, the mission of theological libraries is to preserve, transmit, and advance theological knowledge. Undoubtedly, seminary libraries have contributed immensely to the growth, spiritual formation, and ministerial training of pastors, evangelists, and ministers. The collections of historical and current theological works available in seminary libraries are of great importance for theological education.

Reference collections provide background and historical information for further research in any discipline. The reference collections in a seminary library include commentaries, encyclopedias, handbooks, dictionaries, atlases, and other multi-volume works which cover biblical, theological, and historical topics. Exorbitant prices, limited finances for acquisition, and non-availability of reference works are some of the challenges librarians need to overcome while adding reference works. Small seminaries in the majority world often find it especially challenging to add to their core collections of reference works. Meeting such challenges requires clarity, careful planning, and support from administration and faculty members. Clearly defining the intended use of reference collections in libraries will help librarians proactively develop them (Colson 2007, 174) and make it easier to solicit support from faculty and administrators.

Theological libraries have an important role in supporting the academic programmes offered by seminaries. Irrespective of the size of the seminary or level of education offered by it, the library exists and grows with the institution. Hence, the institutional growth plan should include library development. A seminary library is as important a place of learning as the chapel and classroom, due in no small part to the reference collections held in the library that offer historical and background research information. Although it is an undeniable fact that theological libraries significantly contribute to the spiritual formation of students and faculty, there is a general tendency, prevalent among seminary leaders, to make library development a lower priority compared to building offices and classrooms. It is important for the seminary's administration to include librarians, especially while planning and developing the library. The library should get its allocation of funds from institutional operational budgets. Any compromise on funding allocation for library acquisitions would lead to scarcity of learning resources for students and create a pedagogical vacuum (Lincoln 2004, 7).

Overcoming Challenges to Reference Collection Development

Small seminaries in the majority world often face challenges in meeting their operational costs and their obligations to hold a huge number of donated books regardless of relevance or usefulness. Lack of budget provisions for acquisitions for the reference collection, absence of a collection development policy, and inadequately trained librarians are some of the problems faced by small seminary libraries in the majority world.

Theological libraries and librarians face the herculean task of developing a seminary library collection able to provide resources for the growth and development of scholarly productivity among faculty members and students. No library can afford to procure all resources needed by its users. One of the major reasons seminary administrators and librarians seek to develop their library resources is to meet the requirements set by the accreditation agencies.

Library resources are added not just to fulfill the standards of accreditation bodies but also to meet the needs of newly introduced academic degree programs and courses. According to Dr. Ranganathan's fifth law of library science, the library is a growing organism. It grows in terms of resources added to the library to meet the information needs of an increasing and diverse number of users. It is agreed that most academic libraries were shaped by the research needs of their faculties (Nichols and Rumsey 2001, 19).

There are challenges in developing library reference resources. As we know, majority-world theological seminary libraries face more financial challenges compared to their counterparts in North America and elsewhere. Due to the scarcity of funds, seminaries often operate in maintenance mode, which results in allocating less funding or no funding for the library's acquisitions budget. Lack of support from faculty members can be another disadvantage for librarians seeking to acquire reference works, since faculty members' suggestions are critical in identifying resources for each field of study. Collaboration with faculty members is thus very important.

Theological library staff play an important role in achieving the collection development goals of the library, so any lack of awareness, technical skills, and cooperation among the library staff would derail such development.

Reference Works in Print versus Electronic Format

Libraries must navigate the challenge of providing necessary reference works while also handling the changing information needs of patrons and their access to the available resources. Library administrators should decide whether to acquire reference works in print and/or in electronic format. Based on his survey, Lincoln (2013, 42) observes that most of the instructors and students from Atla-affiliated libraries prefer reference works and bible commentaries in electronic format. Providing reference works in electronic format is convenient for users who can access them from anywhere. They are easy to search to locate relevant information, and they do not cause any storage problems. On the other hand, print reference sources may be less expensive compared to those in electronic format. However, library users often need to spend considerably more time to search and locate information from print reference works. Adequate internet connections, desktop computers, and network facilities should be developed to provide electronic reference works for libraries.

Librarians, in consultation with the faculty members, must carefully plan what type of reference resources should be provided in print and/or online/digital format. Decisions must be made while keeping in mind current users' needs and academic programmes' requirements.

Low-cost Electronic Resources

Ease of search and retrieval of content and remote access are reasons for an increased demand for access to electronic resources by academicians. Subscribing to online electronic resources can be a challenge for libraries with limited finances. The following are some low-cost options for providing access to online theological resources.

The Global Digital Theological Library (GDTL) has an online library that offers subscriptions to majority-world libraries for a small fee calculated according to FTE. The GDTL provides access to e-books, journal articles, and other open access repositories. The Christian Library Consortium (CLC) of the Association of Christian Librarians (ACL) occasionally offers special or discounted e-book packages from various publishers. While considering e-book packages, libraries need to choose whether a single-user or unlimited-user license would be more feasible financially. Through its CLC arrangement, SAIACS was able to add e-book titles to its collection in 2010. It was undoubtedly a step forward for the South Asia Institute of Advanced Christian Stuides (SAIACS) library to subscribe to JSTOR, Bloomsbury Collections, and the GDTL to enhance the availability of learning resources. Atla's special pricing policy for majority-world libraries has enabled SAIACS to subscribe to the Atla Religion Database with Serials.

Open Access Resources

Librarians can prepare and regularly update a list of freely available open access electronic resources, which can complement print collections available in the library. This helps libraries to support the growing information needs of faculty members and students. Faculty members and students can be encouraged to become individual members of the Internet Archive, an online library that allows its members to access thousands of digitized books through a controlled digital lending (CDL) programme. The Open Access Digital Theological Library (OADTL) curates electronic resources available in the field of religion, theology, philosophy, and other related disciplines from various open access online repositories and other digital libraries. Content available in the OADTL can be of great value to the library patrons without any financial impact on the library budget. Regular user education and awareness training programmes offered by libraries will help improve access to the open access content (Sellan and Sornam 2017, 98).

Donations

The Theological Book Network (TBN), Langham Literature Trust, and many other organizations support majority-world libraries by facilitating redistribution of donated books. Another way to strengthen library collections is to contact retired or retiring professors whose personal library collections will be advantageous in filling gaps in the library's collection. These personal library donations carry on the legacy of professors and missional leaders. At the same time, libraries should not become a dumping place for unwanted donations of non-academic materials. To avoid space problems, libraries should accept only a limited number of books of fiction, biographies, and devotional literature. The collection development policy must explicitly specify how to handle donations and include guidelines in accepting and acknowledging donations received from individuals.

Interlibrary Loan and Regional Collaborative Initiatives

Local and regional library networks can be of great help in improving access to resources for patrons. Libraries do not need to invest in rarely used resources that can be either borrowed or consulted through library networks. Librarians can engage in dialogue with other colleagues in the region to form mutually beneficial networks for sharing resources and services. Libraries can mutually agree to avoid redundancy in their collections and focus on developing core collections of reference works. Regionally published literature offers background information for study of culture and ministry of a particular context. Therefore libraries must make efforts to acquire indigenous publications such as souvenirs, newsletters, and journals to preserve and strengthen the reference sources published locally which are otherwise not available from other libraries.

Suggestions

Developing reference collections in small seminaries requires support from administrators, faculty members, and librarians. Regular evaluation of learning resources available online and in print will help librarians assess the relevance and usefulness of such collections. Theological librarians need to be proactive in collaborating with faculty members and research scholars to identify their current research needs and familiarize themselves with trends in research and publishing. Librarians should also explore the possibilities of becoming members of local, regional, national, and international theological librarians' forums for mutual benefit. Librarians also need to keep themselves abreast of developments in the LIS profession.

The following are a few suggestions for growing and improving resources, particularly reference sources, available in small seminaries:

1. In consultation with faculty members and the library committee, formulate a collection development policy which reflects the mission and vision of the institution.

2. Evaluate the present reference collection in light of plans to introduce changes in the curriculum.

3. Assess whether the existing collection needs any weeding to keep the collection more relevant and useful.

4. Collaborate and partner with faculty members to identify gaps in the subject areas of library reference collections and add reference collections based on the input received from them (Sellan 2021, 9). Such collaboration with faculty members is one of the keys for effective collection development (Cooper et al. 2017).

5. Seek partnerships with parent institutions and other theological colleges for collection development and resource sharing in order to reduce the financial burden on the individual libraries (Reekie 2010, 207).

6. Ascertain the faculty members' perception of the adequacy of small libraries' collections and instill in them an awareness

of the importance and usefulness of their input in improving the library collections (Bidlack 2007, 59).

7. Focus more on current curricular and research needs rather than planning for future needs.

8. Consult with colleagues in other libraries to learn from their experiences.

Conclusion

The quality of theological education depends on the quality of learning resources available in seminary libraries. Library collections add value to the programs offered by seminaries. Hence, developing a reference collection in a seminary library is an important task that requires careful evaluation, systematic planning, reasonable funding, emphasis on acquisition of regional publications, and collaboration with faculty members and other networks. A well curated reference collection focuses on academic needs of faculty members and students and plays an important role in the library's service to theological education.

Works Cited

Bidlack, Beth. 2007. "Faculty-Librarian Collaboration and Collection Development Policies: Three Experiences in Different Contexts." *Atla Summary of Proceedings* 61: 58–61.

Colson, Jeannie. 2007. "Determining Use of an Academic Library Reference Collection." *Reference & User Services Quarterly* 47, no. 2: 168–75. *https://doi.org/10.5860/rusq.47n2.168*.

Cooper, Danielle, Roger Schonfeld, Richard Adams, Matthew Baker, Nisa Bakkalbasi, John Bales, Rebekah Bedard, et al. 2017. "Supporting the Changing Research Practices of Religious Studies Scholars." *Ithaka S+R. https://doi.org/10.18665/sr.294119*.

Hattendorf, Lynn C. 1989. "The Art of Reference Collection Development." *RQ* 29, no. 2: 219–29. *https://jstor.org/stable/25828490*.

Kansfield, Norman J. 1980. "Goals for Small Theological Libraries: Section A: Setting Realistic Goals, How to Address Research Needs." Atla Summary of Proceedings 34: 83–5.

Lincoln, Timothy Dwight. 2004. "What's A Seminary Library For?" *Theological Education* 40, no. 1: 1–10. *https://ats.edu/uploads/resources/publications-presentations/theological-education/2004-theological-education-v40-n1.pdf#page=13*.

———. 2013. "Reading and E-reading for Academic Work: Patterns and Preferences in Theological Studies and Religion." *Theological Librarianship* 6, no. 2: 34–52. *https://theolib.atla.com/theolib/article/view/293*.

Nichols, Stephen G., and Abby Smith Rumsey, eds. 2001. *The Evidence in Hand: Report of the Task Force on the Artifact in Library Collections. Optimizing Collections and Services for Scholarly Use.* Washington, D.C: Council on Library and Information Resources.

Reekie, Carol Susan. 2010. "The Theological College Library: An Investigation into Its Role in Ministerial Education and Training." PhD diss., Loughborough University. *https://dspace.lboro.ac.uk/dspace-jspui/handle/2134/8020*.

Sellan, Yesan. 2021. "Partnerships and Collaboration." In *Best Practice Guidelines for Theological Libraries Serving Doctoral Programs*, edited by Katharina Penner, 9–11. ICETE Series. Carlisle: Langham Global Library.

——— and S. Ally Sornam. 2017. "Awareness and Use of Open Access Scholarly Publications among Theological Faculty Members in Karnataka: A Study." *International Journal of Library and Information Science* 6, no. 5: 90–9. *https://iaeme.com/MasterAdmin/Journal_uploads/IJLIS/VOLUME_6_ISSUE_5/IJLIS_06_05_009.pdf*.

Stephens, Myka Kennedy. 2016. "The Future of the Small Theological Library." *Theological Librarianship* 9, no. 1: 28–32. *https://doi.org/10.31046/tl.v9i1.411*.

CHAPTER 9

Developing Future-proof Library Collections

The Case of International Baptist Theological Study Centre

PIETER VAN WINGERDEN

*L*IBRARIES HAVE OFTEN BEEN A CENTRAL ELEMENT IN A RESIDENTIAL COMMUNI-ty of seminary students. It is not uncommon for seminaries with on-site living arrangements to provide access to the library to residential students around the clock. Especially in facilities with shared dormitories, the library can be a haven of rest for students in search of physical space and headspace for reading, writing, and studying. Many a seminary student will have fond memories of working in peace and quiet in secluded corners in the library. By providing these arrangements, the library fulfilled its mission of providing the students that they serve with the resources they need to complete their studies.

And then the pandemic struck. Students were forced to socially distance from each other. Many libraries closed their on-site facilities and limited lending services. Sometimes students were locked down into their dormitories, or even sent home. For many this was an unmitigated disaster. If we can identify one thing that the pandemic did for seminaries worldwide, it was to highlight the importance of digital resources for seminary students.

With the experience of the pandemic fresh in our minds, many seminary libraries have been forced into forward thinking more quickly than normally would have happened. Confronted with the problems of only having limited electronic resources, many libraries had to scramble to provide at least a rudimentary service to their students. As a result, in many libraries, a process of evaluation and strategic planning for the future has now started. As many workplaces in the Western world move towards a more blended way of working, seminary libraries will have no choice but to follow suit if they want to remain relevant. As the community of distance-learning students continues to grow, seminary libraries have received a much-needed prod from the pandemic towards more innovative and future-proof thinking.

In what follows, I will first describe how my own institution, the International Baptist Theological Study Centre (or IBTS for short), has diversified its collection by formulating separate goals for our print and electronic holdings. I will then look at the impending paradigm shift from print-centered to digital-centered collections and suggest strategic ways forward to catalyse the change that many seminary libraries see on the horizon and may have no choice but to adopt.

The Case of IBTS

Our institution said farewell to our residential community when we moved from Prague, Czech Republic, to Amsterdam, the Netherlands, in July 2014. When I started at IBTS in August 2014, we were initially very busy with just finding our feet as a newly established Dutch organisation with a wider European inheritance. As the future of the institution as a whole was getting clearer, it became obvious that changes were required in our library setup in order to serve our students well. In Prague, we had acquired a small, albeit good, selection of electronic resources, some of which were not transferable to the Netherlands due to consortium mismatches. An analysis of our patron groups showed that the library services offered to our main target group (our distance-learning doctoral students) needed some drastic changes in order to justify the existence of the print library. What is the use of a library when it cannot serve its main target group? In the search for a solution, I encountered the Digital Theological Library, which we joined in 2016, within half a year of its going live. The DTL currently provides our students with access to over 600,000 e-books and millions of articles, a staggering number that far surpasses the amount of resources held by almost any seminary library in the world.

After having taken care of our immediate need, we still had a print collection to consider. Our distance-learning students were (and still are) well-served by the electronic holdings of the Digital Theological Library, so the print collection was looking for its own right to exist. Fortunately, our denominational affiliation and the unique international identity of our institution provided us with a clear future. Even though the Angus Library and Archives at Regent's Park College, Oxford, and the Oncken Archiv in Elstal, Germany, have collections that supersede their national contexts, we are the only truly international Baptist institution in Europe and as such can be considered to be a veritable treasure chest of Baptist studies. Even though much of our material may not be unique or rare, the fact that it is held in a single collection makes our library collection unique and rare. As such, it was a very easy choice to bask in our strengths, designate our print collection as an international Baptist research library, and use our acquisitions budget solely to enhance our niche specialty of Baptist and Anabaptist Studies. Our specialty became our strength. The reason for the continued existence of our print library is that we offer an in-depth and unique collection of materials found in no other place in Europe under one roof.

A Paradigm Shift

In the aftermath of, or perhaps still in the midst of, the pandemic, many seminary libraries will see themselves faced with the same conundrum that I encountered when I started at IBTS. Many seminary libraries, however, may be unprepared to answer the main question asked by the pandemic: How can we best serve our student community when the need for access to the print collection is no longer self-evident? The answer to this question is really quite simple, but at the same time of such magnitude that it requires a paradigm shift in seminary libraries: our electronic holdings should take the place of print holdings and become our main resource collection for our students. This requires two major changes in a classic seminary library setup: first, we need to grow our electronic holdings exponentially and sustainably; second, we need to seriously consider the purpose of our library space and our print collection. In what follows I will consider these two changes and identify some ways forward for seminary libraries who are willing to face this impending paradigm shift that the pandemic has forced upon us.

Growing Electronic Holdings

As demand for electronic resources increases, libraries are going to run into two major hindering factors. Since we have relied on our print collections for so long, it is financially impossible for a single seminary library to duplicate its entire print collection in electronic format. In addition, copyright limitations and publisher strategies will often make it impossible to legally acquire electronic versions of required textbooks, even if the financial means were available. For both of these hindering factors, our colleagues in the field have found excellent solutions to counteract this on a large scale.

Counteracting Financial Limitations

Since electronic holdings in libraries have only existed for just a couple of decades, it is no surprise that they have not reached the same maturity as our print holdings that have often existed for many decades or even centuries. In most cases it is not possible for a single library to organise the required financial investment to bring its electronic holdings up to level with its print holdings. The only way forward is cooperation. The Digital Theological Library (DTL) is an example of what this could look like. The traditional model for a library is to license or purchase electronic material themselves directly from the publisher, making these holdings available to their own patrons. The DTL is a very different type of model: it is a born-digital library that is co-owned by a limited number of institutions. These co-owning institutions each contribute towards the annual budget that is used to fund operating costs (staff and electronic systems) and to acquire or licence electronic materials from publishers and vendors. These electronic holdings are then made available to the patrons of the co-owning institutions. My own institution (IBTS) does not own electronic holdings but, because we are a co-owner of the DTL, our students have access to the entire electronic holdings it offers. The annual acquisitions budget of the DTL exceeds our full annual library budget, which only goes to show that it would have been impossible for us as a small institution to provide our patrons with access to the same amount and quality of electronic holdings as the DTL is now doing for us. Without cooperation, we would have had to seriously question the viability of our small institution for our small group of distance-learning postgraduate students.

Counteracting Copyright Limitations and Publisher Strategies

Any librarian who has ever worked in electronic acquisitions will know that publications will not always be available for library purchase. Sometimes they are tucked away in expensive packages, sometimes the publisher is not very good with offering electronic resources, sometimes a publication is too old. In the past, this meant that it was impossible to acquire this publication in electronic format for our library collection. Nowadays, fortunately, a solution has been found for this problem that works in tandem with US copyright: controlled digital lending (CDL). The principle is that a library is allowed to digitise a publication, put the print copy in permanent storage, and then circulate the digitised version in their electronic library in a controlled system, thus allowing only one electronic copy to be put on loan against every print copy held in storage. This will allow seminaries with specific denominational courses to make older and niche material available to their students in electronic format. The most conspicuous example of this is the Books To Borrow collection of the Internet Archive, which at the time of writing already contains over three million volumes and is steadily growing. The DTL has integrated CDL into their holdings and has set up a digitisation programme of their own. Discussions on the legality of CDL in a non-US context are ongoing, but the principle has been embraced by the International Federation of Library Associations (IFLA), who argue that "there is a strong socio-economic case for enabling Controlled Digital Lending in libraries around the world."

Repurposing Library Space and Print Collections

So, what happens to the print holdings once our electronic holdings provide our students with what they need to complete their studies successfully? This is a difficult and confrontational question in the light of the personal attachment that many seminary administrators, librarians, and students often have to their library space and print collection. If we accept the necessity of the paradigmatic shift towards making our electronic holdings the main set of resources with which we serve our mission as theological libraries, this may lead some to the point of view that a seminary does not need a library if it can tap into the collections of projects like the Internet Archive Books To Borrow section of the DTL. However much it pains a librarian to admit this, in some cases this will be the only viable option for a seminary. The print collection could be donated to the DTL or to the Internet Archive for inclusion in their CDL programmes so that the material will still remain accessible to the future students of the seminary.

However, we must not overlook the continuing strength of the library space and its quiet working spaces for a residential student community. For seminary libraries with a secure future and a largely residential community, it could be enough to adjust the balance between print and electronic acquisitions in favour of the latter and to continue to use the library space as a haven of rest where quiet study is made possible. For seminary libraries with a gradually growing and largely non-residential community, it might be wiser to limit the acquisition goals of the print collection and choose a clear focus. Some may want to focus on strengthening their reference collection, while others may want to specialise in a certain theological topic in line with their identity. The strength and weaknesses of the existing print collection should be analysed in order to identify the most relevant section or topic. If there is ample space, it might not be immediately necessary to weed the existing print collection, but it might be an intentional choice of a seminary that has chosen a clear focus for their print collection to transition older parts not consistent with the new focus into a CDL collection. Should library space be an issue, then the argument is stronger to convert stacks into study space by donating parts of the print collection to the DTL, the Internet Archive, or another CDL partner.

Conclusion

Even before the pandemic, our institution proved that it is possible and beneficial to fully embrace the described paradigm shift. International cooperation and creative thinking have substantially changed the playing field and made it possible for IBTS to have a pandemic-proof library in place even before we had contemplated the possibility of a pandemic. As the pandemic will undoubtedly fade away at some point, it would seem easy for seminary libraries with a residential student community to quickly revert to business as usual, especially since a paradigm shift is never an easy thing to live through. In many cases, it will be difficult to garner support among seminary administrators and even librarians. However, I would argue that the benefits of cooperative projects, the progressively more blended nature of Western work experiences, and the developments in education towards less residential and more distance-learning programmes will eventually force us all into this paradigm shift, whether we want to accept it or not. Since the pandemic has not been a pleasant experience for any of us, it is better to let such a paradigm shift happen on our own terms than to be caught on the back foot again. I hope that the strategic ways forward that I have sketched in this chapter will be of assistance to my colleagues worldwide as we try to come to terms with a changing library landscape in order to lead our libraries into the future.

Works Cited

Archive.org. "Books to Borrow." Accessed December 1, 2021. *https://archive.org/details/inlibrary.*

Controlleddigitallending.org. "Controlled Digital Lending By Libraries." Accessed December 1, 2021. *https://controlleddigitallending.org.*

Digital Theological Library. Accessed December 1, 2021. *https://libguides.thedtl.org/home.*

IFLA. 2001. "Guidelines for a Collection Development Policy Using the Conspectus Model." Accessed December 1, 2021. *https://repository.ifla.org/handle/123456789/52.*

———. 2021. "IFLA Position on Controlled Digital Lending." Accessed December 1, 2021. *https://ifla.org/publications/ifla-statement-on-controlled-digital-lending.*

Wingerden, Pieter van. 2021. "'A Missionary in and of Itself': The John Smyth Library of the International Baptist Theological Study Centre (Amsterdam)." In *Best Practice Guidelines for Theological Libraries Serving Doctoral Programs,* edited by Katharina Penner. Carlisle: Langham Global Library.

CHAPTER 10

Developing Special Collections & Archives at General Theological Seminary Post-pandemic

MELISSA CHIM

A T GENERAL THEOLOGICAL SEMINARY, THE PANDEMIC HAS BROUGHT ABOUT AN opportunity to rethink our collection policy with regard to our special collections and institutional archive. With the move to the remote classroom, my manager and I had to make sure the archives were accessible to students who could not return to campus. We also anticipate that our library will expand its digital resources, most notably student theses and administrative documents. As we move forward in updating our collection policy, we will also have to rethink our access policy too.

The General Theological Seminary was founded in 1817 by the General Convention of the Episcopal Church and is located in the Chelsea neighborhood of New York City. The seminary, on average, has about forty to sixty graduates per year. The Christoph Keller Jr. Library (CKJL) is home to a rich theological collection and an archive that also serves as an institutional repository. As the reference librarian and archivist, I have the wonderful opportunity to help students access and interpret our collections.

Prior to the COVID-19 pandemic, our archives collection development policy focused on accessioning sources related to theological research. During the pandemic, my manager and I worked from home from March to September 2020, where we answered reference requests pertaining to the special collections virtually. I also hosted multiple webinars that allowed my students to access our special collections from off campus. As the end of the pandemic comes within reach, we will update our collection development policy to reflect our student and faculty needs. Additionally, the transition of our president will bring in new material that will be our first processed archival collection since the pandemic began.

Similar to many small theological libraries, the CKJL wears many hats in order to meet the needs of its patrons both on and off campus. Its main collection comprises both print and electronic resources related to theological research, particularly the history of Anglicanism and the Episcopal Church. It also boasts a reference collection comprising commentaries, encyclopedias, atlases, and similar materials. Other themes actively collected by the library include liturgics, patristics, spirituality, ethics, and ecumenics. Although the primary language of the library's collection is English, Western European languages and ancient languages such as Hebrew, Greek, and Latin are also prioritized.

The library's special collections and archives serve as both a repository for materials of historic value and as an institutional records repository. Due to the library's size and budget limitations, artifacts related to the seminary are housed in the special collections room, which comprises about 150 linear feet of material. One can find a 15th-century book of hours not far from a copy of the seminary's 1850 board of trustees minutes. Prior to the pandemic, the library did not house electronic copies of institutional material such as student dissertations or seminary newsletters. Our collection policy was last updated in 2014.

Before the pandemic, our special collections received a lot of interest from faculty and students. The library's Books of Common Prayer and Hebrew scrolls are the most often requested items. This is in conjunction with two of the most popular courses, which are History of the Prayer Book and Old Testament. The two instructors of those courses schedule a visit once a semester where students are encouraged to have hands-on interaction with these materials. I use class visits like these to advertise our special collections and let students pursuing a thesis know that they are welcome to use the archives for their research.

Additionally, we keep a four-case exhibit open to view in our main reading area. We change this exhibit every three months and use items of interest from the archives. For example, we display many copies of the poem "'Twas the Night before Christmas" (written by General Theological Seminary professor Clement C. Moore) during the Christmas season.

With the onset of the pandemic, the library's approach to its special collections department had to evolve to meet the needs of a now completely virtual seminary community. Since the students could not come to the special collections, I wanted to bring the special collections to them. I presented two webinars during the pandemic: one webinar was on the history of female students at the seminary in honor of Women's History Month (which was recorded and is currently available to view), and the second was on the seminary's response to the 1918 flu pandemic and both world wars (not recorded). These were both scheduled to coincide with breaks in the class schedule. Before transitioning to working from home, I took photographs of the special collections materials for each presentation and incorporated them into PowerPoint presentations.

My webinar on the history of women at the seminary focused on four groups: historically significant women in the Episcopal Church (such as Florence Li Tim Oi), the first female students at General (Peggy Muncie, Paige Bigelow, and later Pauli Murray), the first female faculty members (Dora Chaplin), and the campus wives' group known as the Women of General. I used photographs and documents from the special collections, including a copy of *Dark Testament* signed by Pauli Murray. I also included interviews I conducted over email from former members of the Women of General group. Since the webinar took place over Zoom, students were muted and could only pose questions in the chat function.

My second webinar, however, was presented in Zoom's classroom mode and allowed students to participate more easily. This webinar focused on the seminary during the 1918 flu pandemic and both world wars. Most of the sources I used came from our board of trustees minutes. I discovered that, contrary to what I expected, the seminary was in favor of students engaging in military service rather than acting as conscientious objectors. I also included photographs in my presentation, notably of student Paul Ken Imai, a Japanese student who graduated in 1942 and later worked with congregations affected by Japanese internment. Both webinars ultimately had an equal amount of both students and faculty attending.

The greatest challenge in presenting these webinars was the inability to encourage students to physically interact with the historical materials on display. One way to overcome this challenge in the future is to incorporate video of the archival material into a PowerPoint presentation. For example, I can record myself opening a book so students can experience the sound of the pages turning and the spine cracking. They will also be able to see how the paper has aged over time. Although this will not fully replicate the ability to touch an object, showing students video footage will allow them to engage with the special collections while attending class virtually. I plan to utilize these techniques for the 2022–2023 year.

As the pandemic draws to a close and we transition back to working physically in the library, we will revisit our collection development policy regarding our special collections. This change is also very timely as the seminary transitions to a new president. The papers I received from the retiring president are the first collection I will process post-pandemic. As a small library, our special collections room also serves as our institutional repository. One major change brought about by the pandemic is revisiting the question of acquiring a digital repository.

In addition to processing this new collection, the library no longer requires students to submit bound copies of their theses before graduation. As of summer 2020, students submit a PDF of their finished thesis to both the library and registrar's office. Additionally, many of the physical materials within the president's papers are available electronically. One major challenge of having a combined special collections and institutional repository is physical space. A digital repository will relieve this burden, but questions of cost, technology (such as using a cloud-based repository), and sustainability also arise.

Another consideration when updating our policy will be with regards to content. Our current policy states that "The Library Archives does not have space for, and thus cannot receive reprints, bulky artifacts, or more than two copies of reports and publications" (see appendix). Transitioning to an electronic repository might open the library to the possibility of having multiple copies of a document. Routine correspondence and announcements, which are currently not accepted into the archive, may have a place in a digital archive.

With regards to the retiring president's papers I am going to process, having a digital repository would allow me to keep both hard and electronic copies of the president's correspondence. Ideally, a digital repository will be a supplement to, rather than a full replacement of, our special collections and archives room.

Another concern when updating our collection development policy with regards to the institutional repository is access. Prior to the pandemic, students, faculty, and board members had complete open access to the institutional repository collection. Researchers from outside the seminary were required to fill out a research request form and generally have open access to institutional records. Requests for institutional records after 2010, however, are directed to the president on a case-by-case basis. In light of the incoming president's papers and student theses being mostly in electronic form, the library will have to consider how to develop a new access policy for digital materials. As conversations about digital repositories continue, my manager and I will keep these materials on the library's server and grant access as needed.

The Christoph Keller Jr. Library's archives collection development policy reflects the educational needs of the seminary community. The COVID-19 pandemic has inspired the library to update its policy to make the archives and special collections accessible to students and faculty engaging in virtual classrooms. Transitioning to a digital repository will bring both opportunities and challenges, particularly in light of the first collection I will process post pandemic. Consequently, the library's collection policy must evolve to preserve the seminary's heritage into the future.

Appendix: Collection Development Policy of the General Theological Seminary

As a rule, General Theological Seminary institutional records are considered by the Library Director to be appropriate for the Archives when they document policy development and precedents, major projects, or university rights and responsibilities; if their subject matter caused considerable comment on the Close or in the media; if they involved litigation or large sums of money; or, if they have been vital to the operation or spiritual life of the Seminary. Materials such as grant applications are to be considered for inclusion, as they often contain historical narratives and statistics and other related materials that can be useful for researchers.

Institutional materials considered by the Library Director for archival status include:

- Correspondence and subject files of the Dean, President and Seminary administration.

- Publications, such as newsletters and annual reports.

- Records of program or curriculum development.

- Departmental minutes; committee minutes and reports.

- Self-studies, histories, and accreditation reports.

- Records about symposia and special projects.

- Records about cooperative efforts with other institutions.

- Records about relationships with government, business, or industry.

- Photographs (if identified).

- Faculty materials, including papers and selected publications.

The Seminary Records Retention Guidelines are used by individual departments to determine whether administrative or transactional records and documents should be retained or destroyed. Library staff is available to assist individual departments in evaluating their non-current files and determining whether they are appropriate for the Library Archives.

The following guidelines are intended to be helpful for departments with institutional records they identify as having possible archival value. The Library Archives does not have space for, and thus cannot receive reprints, bulky artifacts, or more than two copies of reports and publications. Routine correspondence (for example, requests for course information and acknowledgments) is generally not valuable, nor are announcements, directives, and other memoranda distributed to the Seminary as a whole.

The Archives does not accept records in hanging files or looseleaf binders; nor are loose, unfoldered papers received. These should be re-foldered into manila folders. Records of distinct offices, committees, or organizations should not be intermixed. Records that are soiled, moldy or identified as having environmental damage should be photocopied and the originals discarded or sealed and preserved, according to their value.

The transfer of records from offices and departments of the Seminary to the Archives is considered permanent. When files and office materials are transferred to the Archives, they become part of the Library's Special Collections and are made available to staff and patrons only in the Special Collections room of the Library, with access subject to Library policy. Offices and departments are advised to ensure that they have no current or frequent need for any records intended for transfer. These records are subject to the same terms and conditions of use and reproduction as other items that form part of the Library's Special Collections.

CHAPTER 11

Collaborative Collection Development

Opportunities and Challenges

KERRIE BURN

C OLLABORATIVE COLLECTION DEVELOPMENT AMOUNTS TO GOOD STEWARDSHIP OF library resources, especially when budgets and human re- sources are limited. This chapter will outline some of the many ways that libraries can collaborate in a range of collection de- velopment initiatives. These include: the creation of shared print col- lection policies, retention agreements, shared library systems, joint purchasing of electronic resources, optimization of print journal subscriptions, and reciprocal borrowing agreements. Sharing collec- tions can reduce the need for multiple libraries to purchase the same resource, a particularly useful strategy when libraries are located in close proximity. Users can also benefit from the different collecting priorities of collaborating libraries, with their corresponding sub- ject strengths and areas of teaching or research specialization.

The University of Divinity is an Australian-based ecumenical in- stitution with ten affiliated colleges and fifteen associated libraries.

Founded in 1910, the university is very small compared to most other universities, with approximately 700 full-time-equivalent (FTE) students. It awards certificates and diplomas through to master's and doctoral degrees. The combined collections of University of Divinity Libraries, together with the university's shared online resources, provide staff and students with access to an extensive range of resources that support excellence in learning, teaching, and research. Together, the libraries associated with the university have been able to provide access to a greater range of resources, certainly more than any one library could provide alone. Some of the projects that have been successfully implemented at the university are detailed below, and these will hopefully serve as a model for other libraries to emulate, learn from, or adapt for their own purposes.

The Foundations of Collaborative Collection Development

The libraries associated with the University of Divinity have several formal agreements in place that provide the foundation for successful collaborative collection development activities.

The Library Hub (2015)

The Library Hub (*library.divinity.edu.au*) provides all members of the university with a single point of access to online databases and e-books, and a range of other useful links and academic resources. The Library Hub was launched in February 2016 with the aim of creating a consistent standard of access for all staff and students, regardless of their home college or associated libraries, and to reduce costs and increase resources by using a single license where possible for online resources available to the whole university.

The project was funded under the university's strategic plan and, after a competitive tender process, the project was established through a formal agreement between the University of Divinity and Mannix Library. This agreement authorises the Mannix Library manager to liaise with vendors on behalf of the university and to liaise with libraries associated with the university to maximise the benefits of the Library Hub. Arrangements made under the agreement are reviewed annually, providing an opportunity to note ongoing projects to grow and improve the Library Hub, document targets for the following year, and revise the annual budget.

The creation and development of the Library Hub is an ongoing collaborative library project that has demonstrated its value many times over. This was particularly evident during the rapid transition to online learning and the protracted lockdowns in 2020 and 2021 due to the COVID-19 pandemic. The Library Hub provides access to a much greater range of databases (*divinity.libguides.com/az.php*) and other online resources than any individual library could afford and avoids the need for very small institutions with limited resources to purchase the same online resources. Products such as LibGuides have also been used by the university to centralise library-related information and to produce a range of general purpose and subject-related guides (*divinity.libguides.com*). This has avoided the need for multiple libraries to produce similar material, saving time and creating greater consistency for all staff and students. A single University of Divinity Libraries brochure (*indd.adobe.com/view/432446da-6151-4544-8c3a-256ec177cba1*) also provides summary information about all of the library collections and resources to which members of the university have access.

The University of Divinity - Libraries Agreement (2018)

Following the successful establishment of the Library Hub, steps were taken to formalise the relationship between each library and between the university and each library. This was for the purposes of the advancement of scholarship and mutual support, including participation in university governance, the development of policy relating to library resources, reviewing the allocation of funding for libraries, and the development of shared library services and resources for the benefit of all members of the university and users of each library. This formal agreement, which was signed by representatives of participating libraries and the university in December 2018, documents the obligations and commitments of all parties. Under this agreement, each library agrees to:

- provide all staff, students and other members of the university with access to their collections, including borrowing rights, at no charge (subject to reasonable constraints);

- contribute information to and provide reasonable support for the university-wide library catalogue of library resources;

- contribute to supporting the library committee of the university's academic board in the discharge of its responsibilities;

- abide by the Statement of Rights, Responsibilities and Conduct of Members of the University;

- abide by policies of the university that affect libraries and have been established after consultation with the library committee.

In turn, the university agrees to:

- maintain a library committee of the university's academic board and to provide for representation of each library which is party to the agreement on that committee;

- ensure the membership of the academic board includes the chair of the library committee or another suitably qualified librarian;

- consult with the library committee in the development or revision of policies of the university which directly affect libraries;

- reserve a portion of tuition fee income for distribution to libraries;

- ensure that each library which is party to the agreement is eligible to apply for relevant university internal competitive grants such as research grants;

- maintain a digital Library Hub accessible by all students, staff and other members of the university;

- provide each library that is party to the agreement with access to the digital Library Hub, subject to the terms and conditions of contracts with vendors and suppliers to the digital Library Hub.

The Library Collections Policy (2019)

This is an example of one of the policies anticipated in the library obligations section of the University-Libraries Agreement (clause E). The Library Collections Policy (*divinity.edu.au/documents/library-collections-policy*) was created by the library committee and subsequently approved by the university's academic board. The impetus for this policy was the desire to develop a shared retention policy to ensure that no library discarded uniquely held items. However, the policy also outlines a number of general principles to guide collaborative collection development, which are (in part) outlined below.

General Principles

- Catalogued items held by only one library (including different editions) are not discarded but are retained by the original library owner or transferred to another library within the university network.

Principles Guiding Collaborative Collection Development

- All libraries that are signatories of the University Libraries Agreement are guided by a principle of cooperation, and whenever reasonably possible they:
  - agree to provide access and borrowing rights to their libraries to all members of the University of Divinity;
  - provide free interlibrary loans (including cost of postage) to other signatory libraries;
  - support the development of university-wide collection policies and contribute to collaborative collection devel-

opment policy discussions, activities and strategies developed by the library committee;

° contribute to projects associated with special collections held by libraries associated with the university, including linking to these collections via the Library Hub;

° maintain minimum cataloguing standards (as developed by the library committee) to enhance discovery of all library holdings in the university's combined library catalogue, avoid duplication of records, and optimize access to library collections via the Library Hub;

° have an in-principle commitment to making electronic purchases through the Library Hub;

° participate in the e-book purchasing model established for the purpose of purchasing single-title e-books which are then available to all members of the university.

The relationship between the library committee and the academic board ensures that there is good representation from multiple stakeholders across the university in any library-related decisions. Having formal library policies that are developed by the library committee but approved/authorized and subsequently reviewed by the academic board ensures that there is greater buy-in at all levels of the institution and affirms a commitment to the stewardship of the combined resources of all libraries. In contrast, the success of any project can be impeded by competing agendas, allegiances, or loyalties to previous partnerships outside the current collaborative network. A formal policy document can help to develop a sense of mutual accountability for the commitments that it records. Having formal agreements in place can be an important prerequisite for successful collaborative projects, ensuring that all libraries (and other institutional stakeholders) have a shared understanding of their responsibilities and entitlements. This in turn can have a positive influence on the culture of the institution if the policies reflect the partners' shared vision, mission and values.

Current Collaborative Activities

The university's library committee meets four times per year and reports directly to the university's academic board. Librarians also hold a "Librarians Day" prior to the start of each academic year to discuss shared activities and priorities for the year ahead.

Shared E-book Purchasing Model (2017)

In 2017, the library committee established a shared e-book purchasing model which enables single title e-books to be purchased centrally and made available via the university's Library Hub. This model is currently opt-in and not all libraries have chosen to participate. A potential barrier to collaboration can occur when not all participants are seen to be contributing equally, with some libraries making minimal contributions while at the same time benefiting significantly from the contributions of others. Despite this, the university's shared e-book purchasing model proved to be extremely beneficial during the COVID-19 pandemic, when there was a rapid transition to online learning and a greater reliance on online resources that could be accessed remotely. Because of the need for increased access to e-books during the pandemic a number of additional libraries chose to participate in the shared system from March 2020.

University ID Card (2017) and Reciprocal Borrowing (2019)

Other current collaborative activities include the production of a single University of Divinity ID card. The provision of this card, which can be used to borrow from all libraries associated with the university, was rolled out across all colleges in 2017. This replaced a system where every library had issued its own borrower's card. In 2019, a reciprocal borrowing arrangement was established between the University of Divinity Libraries and the University of Melbourne, a much larger institution. The University of Divinity ID card can be used as proof of identity at this library.

Shared OCLC WorldShare Management Services (2021)

In early 2021, four libraries associated with the university implemented a shared instance of OCLC's WMS Library Services Platform. This has resulted in a number of significant benefits, including streamlined processes, reduced costs, and improved functionality and collection accessibility. In 2022, three additional libraries will join the shared system, and the hope is that further libraries will choose to do the same over the next few years. Previously, OCLC WorldCat Discovery had been the basis for the university-wide shared catalogue of library print resources. OCLC WorldCat Discovery is now integrated into the Library Hub search interface. It provides access to all of the Library Hub's electronic resources as well as the print holdings of all libraries associated with the university that contribute their holdings to Libraries Australia, the resource sharing service managed by the National Library of Australia. For the libraries that also use the shared OCLC WMS library services platform, live availability data displays in Library Hub search results in addition to basic holdings information. The OCLC infrastructure also includes access to CONTENTdm, which enables the university to showcase digital special collections on a shared platform (*divinity.contentdm.oclc.org*).

Future Collaborative Projects

The library committee established a collection development working group several years ago, but unfortunately its initial work was interrupted by staff changes and the COVID-19 pandemic. The working group was recently reconstituted and will be investigating a number of collaborative collection development opportunities and facilitating future projects.

These could include:

- finalising a collaborative collection development and access policy for University of Divinity libraries;

- investigating further opportunities to reduce duplication of resources across the university;

- reviewing journal subscriptions across all libraries, both print and electronic;

- reviewing the e-book purchasing model and access to e-books across the university;

- making recommendations about collection development policies and best use of University of Divinity funding for library resources, to ensure widest possible access.

Most libraries have their own individual collection development and access policy, and many updated their policies when the working group was first established. The intention now is to develop a collaborative collection development and access policy which will facilitate future collaborative initiatives and formally document its underlying principles, shared understandings, and the commitments of the university and individual libraries. Collection development policies help to ensure that a library meets both the current and future needs of its institution. In addition to identifying current needs, a collaborative collection development policy would therefore seek to identify developing areas of teaching and research at the university. This would assist with determining purchase priorities and ensure that appropriate resources were available when required. The policy would also document decisions such as purchasing preferences for print versus digital formats. Purchasing e-books that are accessible to all members of the university, wherever they are located, can obviously reduce the need for multiple libraries to purchase the same print item.

A collaborative collection development and access policy would also identify the subject strengths of individual library print collections. These areas of specialization may be related to the different emphases of particular denominations, religious orders, or traditions at each institution, the historical teaching and research interests of staff, as well as the library's budget. The policy can document collection strengths across the collaborating libraries and record agreed-to commitments to maintain purchasing in these areas, allowing other libraries to also commit to retaining and building collection strengths in other areas. These mutual commitments can benefit the distributed collection model that operates at the university. The workability of this kind of model depends on the proximity of library collections and ease of access to resources for library users.

A project to evaluate current print and electronic journal subscriptions across the university was proposed in early 2022. This project would ascertain where the same title was held at multiple locations, which titles were available electronically, and where potential gaps exist. A number of libraries have already cancelled their individual journal subscriptions where the full text of a title is available online via the Library Hub's database subscriptions. A future journal optimization project would then seek commitments from individual libraries to retain titles that are not available via the Library Hub (or which have significant embargo periods), which in turn may allow other libraries to cease their own subscriptions. Aggregation of some titles to ensure complete runs of print journals at the one location may also be considered. Final decisions will be based on local requirements, proximity to holdings at other libraries, usage, price, and availability of titles in electronic format. There is also the potential for any cost savings to be re-allocated to the purchase of individual e-journal titles that are not available via any of the Library Hub's current database subscriptions.

Another project that is currently under discussion is a possible shared print repository. This would help to address the space limitations currently faced by some libraries and their resulting inability to significantly grow their physical collections. Relocating items to a shared repository would also help to ensure that the last copy of all items was retained and accessible. Having a documented retention policy also assists libraries whose holdings contribute to the distributed collection. It assists librarians to make decisions about whether to weed or retain items and means that not all libraries need to keep multiple copies of the same title. This sort of collaborative project is initially more likely to be considered for specialist research items rather than standard undergraduate texts. It is important for all stakeholders to be involved in any decision-making processes and for libraries to make informed evidence-based decisions on which monographs to weed, retain, digitize, and/or transfer to a shared repository. Data related to subject coverage, local usage, uniqueness and/or level of duplication, and availability in other local libraries would help to inform group decisions. The new OCLC WMS system currently shared by four libraries has a shared print option which enables a library to commit to retain certain items. This "committed to retain" information can appear on the catalogue display and be easily identified when doing collection analysis such as identifying the areas of duplication across participating libraries.

These kinds of collaborative projects require a great deal of transparency, trust, goodwill, and communication between the participating libraries. These are essential prerequisites for the success of any collaborative collection development initiative. No library wants to cancel a subscription on the basis of another library's commitment to its retention, only to have the second library renege on its agreement, close its doors, or change its institutional affiliation completely. This becomes a risk management issue, and libraries must make decisions based on the best available evidence at the time, perhaps with a back-up contingency plan. Libraries with a history and track record of successful collaborations will obviously feel more confident about making commitments to future shared collection development initiatives. A tension may always exist between the autonomy of an individual library and their commitment to the collaborative work of the larger group. However, the success of previous projects can result in an increased appetite for future projects and a confidence in their likelihood of success.

Conclusion

Collaborative collection development initiatives can be extremely beneficial for participating libraries. Together, libraries can ensure their collective dollars stretch further and provide access to a much greater range of resources than any one library could provide alone. Limited—and in some cases diminishing—library budgets will obviously go further if they are not spent purchasing the same resources as other collaborating libraries or other libraries in close proximity. Collaborative collection development allows libraries to develop individual collection strengths, while the institution's distributed collection as a whole provides access to a more comprehensive and diverse selection of the complete scholarly record. Through a shared vision and an openness to working collaboratively, libraries can significantly enhance the range of resources and services that they offer to their communities.

Works Cited

Association for Library Collections & Technical Services. 2016. *Shared Collections: Collaborative Stewardship.* Edited by Dawn Hale. Chicago: American Library Association.

Burgett, James, Linda L. Phillips, and John M. Haar. 2004. *Collaborative Collection Development: A Practical Guide for Your Library.* Chicago: American Library Association.

Fletcher, Stephanie, Kevin Compton, and Rebecca Miller. 2014. "Toward a Model for Consortial Sharing of E-Books among Theological Libraries." *Theological Education* 48, no. 2: 25–32. Accessed April 20, 2022. *https://ats.edu/uploads/resources/publications-presentations/theological-education/2014-theological-education-v48-n2.pdf.*

Mayer, Robert J. 2018. "Theological Librarians and Collection Management: Collaborative Policy Development." *Theological Librarianship* 11, no. 2: 8–11. *https://doi.org/10.31046/tl.v11i2.530.*

Shelton, Cynthia. 2004. "Best Practices in Cooperative Collection Development: A Report Prepared by the Center for Research Libraries Working Group on Best Practices in Cooperative Collection Development." *Collection Management* 28, no. 3: 191–222. *https://doi.org/10.1300/J105v28n03_02.*

University of Divinity. 2019. "Reciprocal Borrowing Arrangement Established Between the University of Divinity and the University of Melbourne." *Vox,* 3 September. *https://vox.divinity. edu.au/news/reciprocal-borrowing-arrangement-established-between-the-university-of-divinity-and-the-university-of-melbourne.*

———. 2021. "Increase Collaboration and Consistency." *Vox,* August. *https://vox.divinity.edu.au/news/increase-collaboration-and-consistency.*

Contributors

Carisse Mickey Berryhill, PhD, serves as special assistant to the dean for strategic initiatives at Abilene Christian University's Brown Library after 17 years as special collections librarian there. Before coming to ACU, she was associate librarian at Harding School of Theology in Memphis, TN (1992–2004) and professor of English at Lubbock Christian University (1975–1992). Berryhill holds advanced degrees in English, library science, and church history. Berryhill has received ACU's Faculty Service Award (2017) and Pepperdine University's Distinguishwed Christian Service Award for her efforts in preservation of Stone-Campbell history (2011). She has three times received the Excellence in Online Teaching Award from the WISE consortium of library schools for her Theological Librarianship course at the University of Illinois (2007, 2009, 2012). She is chair of the corporation board of *Restoration Quarterly*. She has been an Atla member since 1992.

Kerrie Burn is the library manager at Mannix Library, Catholic Theological College, a member institution of the University of Divinity in Melbourne, Australia. She also manages the university's online Library Hub and is a member of the university's Library Taskforce. Burn is a former member of the Atla International Theological Librarian Education Task Force and a current member of the Atla Board of Directors. Burn has worked in theological libraries for almost 30 years, as well as in library and research support roles in the Australian university sector. She holds a Bachelor of Science degree, a Graduate Diploma in Library and Information Studies and a Master of Arts by research. Her research and publication interests include theological libraries, collaborative collection development, and the management of library special collections. Burn also leads the Australian Women in Religion WikiProject, which aims to create new Wikipedia articles and help address the platform's gender gaps.

Melissa Chim is the reference librarian and archivist at the General Theological Seminary. She also serves as an adjunct professor for courses on research methods and graduate writing. She and Anne Silver were the recipients of the 2021 Atla OER Invention Grant and their textbook, *History of the Center for Christian Spirituality*, will be published in summer 2022.

Anita Coleman, PhD, MSEd, MLIS, is an independent consultant and the founding editor of the Anti-Racism Digital Library. She has been an academic librarian, a researcher and library school faculty at research I universities, and a literary publisher for the voiceless. Coleman's interdisciplinary research in digital libraries, knowledge organization, scholarly communication, and education for the information professions has been published in leading journals and presented to global audiences. In 2007, she received a *Library Journal* Mover and Shaker Award for pioneering open access since 2002 when she established dLIST, the Digital Library of Information Science and Technology. Her book, *Rise, Shine, Be Woke* is a collaborative blend of the lived experiences of diverse Americans and essays about anti-racism.

Ward De Pril is head of KU Leuven Libraries Maurits Sabbe Library, the library of the Louvain Faculty of Theology and Religious Studies (Belgium). The Maurits Sabbe Library houses an extensive collection in the domain of theology and religion (1.3 million volumes) and invests substantially in collection development to cater to the information needs of an international user group of theologians and religious scholars.

Leslie A. Engelson, MLIS, currently serves as professor and metadata librarian at Murray State University (MSU). Prior to her tenure at MSU, she served as technical services librarian at Northwest University, where she managed the collection to support the College of Ministry students, faculty, and curriculum. Leslie taught cataloging and collection management at Murray State University for five years and developed a research guide to support collection evaluation and development (*libguides.murraystate.edu/CEAD*). When she's not trying to organize chaos at work, she submerses herself in the chaos of cats and creative activity associated with quilt-making.

Tammy Johnson, MSLS, is the director of Technical Services, John Bulow Campbell Library at Columbia Theological Seminary.

Elizabeth Leahy is professor of theological bibliography and research at Azusa Pacific Seminary and University in Southern California, serving as a faculty member in the James L. Stamps Theological Library and in the seminary. She has worked in theological librarianship for over 30 years and in this time has begun two theological libraries with small budgets. Additionally, she has written on libraries and technology for the US Department of Education and has been a senior research analyst at the Library of Congress. She is grateful for the wonderful colleagues and collaborative help she has received along the way.

Marta Samokishyn is a collection development and liaison librarian at Saint Paul University (Ottawa, ON, Canada) and a research fellow at BCcampus. She has over 12 years of experience of collection development in an academic library. She holds her MIS degree from the University of Ottawa and is currently in the process of finishing her MA in Learning and Technologies from Royal Roads University (BC, Canada). Her research interests include collection development policy and practice, educational technologies, critical digital pedagogy, and critical information literacy.

Yesan Sellan is chief librarian at South Asia Institute of Advanced Christian Studies (SAIACS), a premier theological institution in South

Asia offering postgraduate and doctoral programs in the field of biblical, theological, and missiological studies. Prior to joining SAIACS, he was a librarian at Serampore College. Yesan holds a master's degree in library information science (MLISc) and a PG Diploma in Library Automation and Networking (PGDLAN). He has 25 years of experience as a theological librarian. He was secretary to the Forum of Asian Theological Librarians (ForATL) and served as executive secretary to the Indian Theological Library Association (ITLA). Yesan has a PhD in Library and Information Science from Bharathidasan University. He is actively involved in development of theological librarianship education through various librarians' forums and library associations. Yesan has published ten articles and several conference papers and book chapters.

Pieter van Wingerden is librarian at the John Smyth Library at the International Baptist Theological Study Center in Amsterdam, the Netherlands.

Jeremy Wallace is the head of Collection, Research, and Engagement Strategies at Princeton Theological Seminary's Wright Library. He holds MDiv and PhD degrees from Princeton Theological Seminary and a Master of Information degree from Rutgers University. He has over fifteen years of experience working in libraries, both academic and public, including six years in collection development. He has taught courses at Kean University, Princeton University, Princeton Theological Seminary, The King's College (NYC), and Northwest University.

www.ingramcontent.com/pod-product-compliance
Lightning Source LLC
Chambersburg PA
CBHW031436270326
41930CB00007B/728